RICKIE
FOWLER

This book is dedicated to Anna Marx, a brilliant editor.

Special thanks: John Blake, Joanna Kennedy, James Hodgkinson, Chris Mitchell and all at John Blake Publishing.

Thanks to: Ben Felsenburg, Adrian Baker, Danny Bottono, Dominic Turnbull, Steven Gordon, Pravina Patel, Martin Creasy, Alex Butler, Colin Forshaw, Roy Stone, Tom Henderson Smith, Alan Feltham, Dave Morgan, Lee Smith, Tony Bethel, David Courtnadge, Mark Fleming, Richard Firth, Tony Grassby and Paul Benbow.

Not forgetting: Angela, Frankie, Jude, Nat, Barbara, Frank, Bob and Stephen, Gill, Lucy, Alex, Suzanne, Michael and William.

RICKIE FOWLER

Par Excellence

Frank Worrall

JOHN BLAKE

Published by John Blake Publishing Ltd,
3 Bramber Court, 2 Bramber Road,
London W14 9PB, England

www.johnblakepublishing.co.uk

www.facebook.com/johnblakebooks ⑪
twitter.com/jblakebooks ⓔ

This edition published in 2015

ISBN: 978 1 78418 328 8

British Library Cataloguing-in-Publication Data:

A catalogue record for this book is available from the British Library.

Design by www.envydesign.co.uk

Printed in Great Britain by CPI Group (UK) Ltd

1 3 5 7 9 10 8 6 4 2

Papers used by John Blake Publishing are natural, recyclable products made from
wood grown in sustainable forests. The manufacturing processes conform to the
environmental regulations of the country of origin.

Every attempt has been made to contact the relevant copyright-holders,
but some were unobtainable. We would be grateful if the
appropriate people could contact us.

CONTENTS

CHAPTER ONE

THE BOY WONDER

The boy who would become the pin-up and great hope of American golf after the dark demise of Tiger Woods was born in Murietta, California, on 13 December 1988. Rod and Lynne Fowler decided to call their baby son Rickie Yutaka Fowler. Rickie was an American name liked by Rod while Yutaka was a nod to Lynne's heritage. She is half-Japanese and half-Navajo and wanted both the Asian and Native American sides to be acknowledged within their family when her only son arrived on the scene. The name Yutaka was especially significant to Lynne as it referenced her father – and Rickie's beloved grandfather – Yutaka Tanaka. Twenty-odd years later Rickie would show just how important the family's origins were to him when he set up a charity foundation in his own name to help Japanese and Native-American communities. That would go down well with his mother who had always taught her boy to be generous of spirit and compassionate and kind to everyone, regardless of race, colour or creed.

And Rickie himself would comment on the second part of his Christian name and why it is so important to him, saying, 'My mom's half-Japanese, my grandpa is full Japanese and his first name is Yutaka, so that's how I got the middle name. And he's the one who got me started in golf. So I'm definitely close with my grandpa.'

Rickie would grow up in an enlightened, gentle atmosphere – what he would later in life term a pleasant, secure 'middle-class' upbringing. He would be very close to his mother – who spent a lot of time at home bringing up him and his younger sister Taylor – and he also very much loved and looked up to his father, who always provided well for his family, working hard to make a success of his trucking business. Lynne would nurture Rickie's spiritual and emotional side while Rod would concentrate on the physical, encouraging his growing son to engage in a variety of sports and outdoor activities. It was the ideal blend to channel their son's talents. Even when he became a world-class golfer, Rickie would still take time out for his Bible study and continue to embrace many other more high-energy activities that the great outdoors had to offer. And Lynne would always be on hand to ferry him around for practice and tournaments when Rod was tied up with business commitments.

His parents were always there for him – to encourage and help him with his decisions – but they never pushed him to do something he didn't want to. They were never members of a golf club; Rickie would learn the game – almost teaching himself – by spending hour after hour on the local driving range. As he got older, Rickie would be accompanied to practices on a voluntary basis by golfing expert Barry McDonnell – and the veteran would spend time helping him to perfect his swing, although Barry would often merely look on and nod or grimace as Rickie learned by trial and error.

And his Japanese grandfather Yutaka also played a key role in his development as a compassionate individual and a world-class sportsman: indeed, Rickie would further elaborate upon how important Yutaka was as a positive force in his life, crediting him with introducing him to golf when he was just three years old! Rickie admitted, 'I started playing when I was three, my grandpa – who is Japanese and married to my grandma who is Navajo – started playing golf at that same time and took me to the driving range. He took me that one time when I was three and that was it. I was off and running from there. I did everything on my own for the most part. My grandparents or parents didn't push me to do anything. They just took me if I wanted to go and if I didn't they didn't take me.'

But Rod and Lynne did have to persuade others to let their son take part in competitions from 'about the age of four' – precisely because he was so young. They told various organisers of events that their son was 'very serious' about his game and that he would bring something to a tournament despite his age. No way would he just turn up and mess about: he would offer up his own love of the game and determination to show he could play it, even as a toddler. Rickie would later tell reporters that he was 'sold on the game' after that first session with his granddad and that his focus became such that some people would inevitably consider him a loner.

'It couldn't be perfected,' he said, adding:

It was a hard sport. It's not a team sport, you can't blame anything on anyone else. You can't blame anything on your clubs, it's kind of just all you. I've loved playing team events with golf but I've always been a little more to myself, not standoffish or anything. I was never a part of any particular group of kids growing up and I got along with everyone. I didn't hang out with certain people or anything, just sort of did my own thing. Kind of what I do on the golf course. My game's not like anyone else's really. I don't really dress like anyone else and I've just kind of always been my own person.

His father's favourite hobby would also have a big impact on the adolescent Rickie. Rod was fanatical about dirt bikes and even won Mexico's Baja 1000 race on a Yamaha two years before Rickie was born. As Rickie grew, he, too, became obsessed with motocross and soon became a dirt-bike fanatic. He loved nothing more than to ride the hills in the desert with his dad – even though he would come off and get bruised. Rod told *Yahoo! Sports*, 'We used to go to the desert and ride. There would be big jumps and he was the first one to hit it. He was unbelievable at riding.' Rod had become friends with motocross champion Jeremy McGrath and the latter was impressed when he saw Rickie ride – indeed, he told Rod the boy could have a big future in the sport. Rickie explained how his love of motocross developed thanks to his father's devotion to it, even telling *GolfDigest.com* in 2010 how Rod still enjoyed the sport's thrills and spills: 'He's still at the track two to three times a week. He got me started riding when I was three. He owns a sand-and-gravel/truck-and-transfer business that he started right out of high school, so he's able to spend a good bit of time with me.'

Rickie also spelt out his belief that dirt tracking helped him to become a top golfer – precisely because it encouraged him to take risks and make speedy decisions. He is renowned as one of the fastest players on the golf circuit and feels that came as a result of having to react quickly when he went out on his bike. He said, 'Motocross made me a bit fearless on the course. I've taken the more conservative route on the bike now, but I'm still taking risks and having fun on the golf course. On a dirt bike, when you're sizing up a jump, you can't have any second thoughts. You have to fully commit. If you don't, a lot of things can go wrong. And when things go wrong on a bike, it's a lot worse than when they go wrong on the golf course. Once you commit, you just go. Same goes for a golf shot.'

But calamity – or, as golfing fans might prefer, the hand

of fate – struck when he was fifteen. One day the teenage Rickie was riding up a hill at speed only to see a young boy trudging up the other side as he started his descent. Rickie managed to swerve and avoid the youngster but paid a heavy personal price. He broke three bones in his right ankle and fractured his left wrist. It was a turning point in his life – from then on he made golf his number-one priority, although he would still ride his bikes in his leisure time.

'I had a crash and I had to make a couple of decisions,' Rickie said. 'I picked golf. I broke my foot in three spots, blew out my knee and decided I'd better stick to golf. I liked being in the air but I loved golf too. My grandpa would take me to the driving range and it didn't take me long to realise I'm a little different with golf. I have an eye for seeing things differently. Somehow I just see shots in my head.'

It would prove the correct choice – indeed, an inspired choice – as Rickie now went on to make his mark as a golfer at Murrieta Valley High School and then at Oklahoma State University. He continued to work almost manically on the driving range to improve his game – putting in the hard hours necessary to fine-tune his performance and develop the skills that would elevate him rapidly in the sport. The more work he put in, the more his talent and confidence increased and soon he was shooting a course-record sixty-two to win a Southern California high-school tournament. He also shot sixty-seven in two different regionals and added a sixty-four to win the state title.

Murrieta's mission statement could have been chosen

especially for Rickie, so much did it reflect the way he would lead his own life – with respect for others and discipline and dedication to his work. Murrieta would urge its pupils to always do things the 'RITE way, the Nighthawk way.' RITE stood for Respect, Integrity, Teamwork and Excellence – to oneself and others. Students at the comprehensive school were also taught to improve themselves the HAWK way – through Hard graft, Analytical thinking, being Worthy citizens and Knowledgeable communicators.

Rickie played for one season at Oklahoma State University and lifted the Phil Mickelson Award as the nation's top freshman in 2007–08. Rickie also earned the right to be named the world's top amateur player for thirty-six weeks in 2007 and 2008 but remained the same down-to-earth, approachable young man he had always been. No way did this early success go to his head. His college coach, Mike McGraw, would later make the point that, for all the supposed flashy clothes and image, he was actually a home-loving boy. McGraw told the *Los Angeles Times*, 'One thing that drew me to him was his unusual attitudes toward golf and life. He has his own little look, edgy, trendy, with his long hair and white belts and tight-fitting shirts. But one of the reasons he came to college here was that the town felt more like home to him.'

Rickie was soon making his name on the international stage too. He was an important player for the Americans in their 2007 Walker Cup win over the UK and Ireland. Rickie and partner Billy Horschel recorded a 2–0 win in the foursomes and Rickie finished 1–1 in the singles, making his overall record 3–1. Rickie beat Lloyd Saltman 5 and 4 in his singles match on the Saturday but lost 3 and 2 to Rhys Davies on the Sunday. The event brought Rickie face to face with the man who would develop into his biggest rival as the years rolled by. Like Rickie, Rory McIlroy was a fresh-faced eighteen-year-old out to make a name for himself but the event held even more significance for Rory as it was played on his home turf at the Royal County Down Golf Club in Northern Ireland. But it would be Rickie who drew first blood. He and Horschel defeated Rory and Jonathan Caldwell 2 and 1 in the Sunday morning foursomes.

In the same year, Rickie also triumphed at the Sunnehanna Amateur tournament in June and the Players' Amateur event the following month.

In 2008 he won the Sunnehanna again and made the cut at the US Open – one of only three amateurs to do so that year. After four impressive rounds, he finished tied-for-sixtieth: an excellent achievement for an amateur player and an indication that he would soon be contemplating stepping out with the big boys on the professional scene. Rickie might have still been only an amateur but he was certainly making a mark. His name was being talked of as a golfer who had the potential to not only step up to the plate as a pro but one who could even be competing for tournaments within a couple of years.

In October 2008 Fowler finished runner-up with his teammates in the Eisenhower Trophy at Royal Adelaide in Australia and emerged as the top individual player. The trophy was won by Scotland, who finished nine shots ahead. It was the first time the Scots had won the event after competing as a part of the Great Britain team until 2000. The US team finished on 11-under-par 569, a result achieved, in the main, by Rickie's superb contribution. His final-round score of two-over-par seventy-five would prove to be his worst of the tournament but for the fourth day it would also prove to be the best score for the American team.

The result highlighted just how far Rickie had come as a player. He was now recognised as one of the top amateur players in the world and his personal success at the Eisenhower – the name under which the men's World Amateur Team Championships is played every two years for four consecutive days – served only to substantiate the growing belief that here was a young man who was good enough to soon be playing golf as a fully-paid-up professional.

The following year he would make his second and final appearance in the Walker Cup for the Americans. He played in four matches and starred and won in four matches – helping America to a fine seven-point victory. The tournament was played on home ground for the American team, at Merion Golf Club in Pennsylvania, and they roared to a most impressive 16½ to 9½ victory for a third consecutive win. Rickie, now twenty, was on top form from the first event on the first day. Along with Bud Cauley, he helped get the hosts off to a flier as they beat Luke Goddard and Dale Whitnell 6 and 5. Then, in the afternoon singles session, Rickie defeated Sam Hutsby 7 and 6.

The next morning Rickie and Bud combined once again and proved too strong for Stiggy Hodgson and Niall Kearney, winning one up. In the afternoon Rickie completed his brilliant weekend's work by beating Matt Haines 2 and 1. The BBC best summed up the convincing nature of the victory achieved by Rickie and his teammates, also pointing out how Rickie himself played a key part towards the end of the tournament. They said, 'With just two points needed, the US saw Scotland's Gavin Dear delay the inevitable by beating Brian Harman 3&2 in the lead-off match. But Rickie Fowler's 2&1 win over Matt Haines got the US back on track before the twenty-year-old [Peter] Uihlein put the result beyond doubt.'

Rickie had thoroughly enjoyed the weekend and explained how it had merely confirmed to him that he had made the right decision to choose golf as a career. It also confirmed in his mind that he had been right to delay turning professional so that he could compete in the Walker Cup for a second and final time. He said:

The whole reason I waited around to turn pro was for this weekend. The days leading up to it and the practice we had was just an awesome experience, and to go 4-0 and get the Cup back, it can't get any better. It's going to be tough to top this weekend.

Over there, we had not won in a while, so that was a pretty big thing for us to go out and get the Cup there. And then here, it was – the whole reason I stayed amateur was to come back and play another, and to play it on our home court, you might say, and have our own fans here. From the experiences that I had in 2007 with those guys on the team, I knew there was a very good chance that I was going to be a leader, and that we would have a bit of a younger team … So like I said, there was no question that I was going to wait around.

But the waiting was now almost over. That year he also finished third in the Sunnehanna – which was maybe a bit of a disappointment given that he had won the event the two previous years. But he did have a lot on his mind, like turning pro and concentrating all his focus and attention on that big transition.

This was a young man who had dedicated himself to his work. Unlike others whose heads were turned by stardom and money, Rickie was never one for nightclubs or getting smashed. He would admit that, as he was growing up, he never had the inclination to drink, smoke or go to clubs to act the 'Big I Am'. His family and his own focus and commitment to his work kept him grounded – as did his religious beliefs and weekly Bible studies. He enjoyed watching videos with his friends and his mum and dad and liked to spend time with his younger sister, Taylor. Taylor, who is a couple of years younger than Rickie, had been majoring in Business Studies as a student at California State University in Fullerton – whose notable alumni include the actor Kevin Costner and singer Gwen Stefani. Away from her studies, she had made a name for herself as a golfer too.

She had become a key member of the university golf team from 2009–2011. In the 09/10 season she played 19 rounds in 7 tournaments for the university's 'Titans' team and had the fourth-best scoring average on the squad at 81.6. In the 10/11 campaign Taylor improved still further, becoming the top scorer for the Titans with an average score of 79.36. And if she needed help, Rickie would be on hand just as his parents and granddad had been for him. He was a great brother – even buying Taylor a new car with some of his 2009/10 earnings after he turned professional. By the fall of 2009 Rickie realised he had gone as far as he could as an amateur: it was time for a brand-new challenge for the young man from southern California. Yes, it was time for the Boy Wonder to turn professional and to take on the big guns of golf.

CHAPTER TWO

MAKING WAVES

After his excellent showing in the 2009 Walker Cup, Rickie was keen to make the step up to becoming a professional. He had supreme self-belief and felt that he had earned the right to turn pro after all the wins, honours and plaudits he had earned as an amateur – culminating in that superb series of four victories in his second Walker Cup. That event concluded on 13 September 2009 and just days later he announced that he had, indeed, finally joined the ranks of the pro game. It wasn't a case of Rickie being arrogant when he said he deserved to be part of the pro circuit – he was, after all, the top-ranked amateur in the world. 'He had served his apprenticeship well and had gone as far as he possibly could in the amateur field,' a golfing insider told me. 'It was definitely time for him to turn pro and no one begrudged him his right to that. He had earned it with the efforts he had put in as an amateur over the years.'

Rickie certainly had earned his elevation and American golf fans were delighted that he was now entering the professional game. They are a knowledgeable lot on that side of the Atlantic when it comes to golf, and I was told that the general feeling was that here, at last, was a youngster who could stir things up among the established order in the US – and could be 'a future superstar in the game'. The pundits hoped he might even play a big part in helping America to retain the Ryder Cup in 2010. They had finally wrested the trophy back off the Europeans in 2008 at the Valhalla Golf Club east of Louisville in Kentucky. It had taken them nine long years to bring the coveted trophy home and every golf lover Stateside was desperate for them not to relinquish their hold on it when the tournament crossed back over the Atlantic to the Celtic Manor resort in Newport, Wales.

There was a definite feeling among seasoned golf watchers in the US that the pendulum was swinging back in Europe's favour and that their boys were clear underdogs. The event was being held on away territory in Europe, and it had been seventeen years since America had last triumphed in that continent. Indeed, US skipper Corey Pavin admitted it would be a struggle to land the trophy for the first time since the Belfry in 1993. Pavin said, 'Given the advantage of playing over in Europe, I think that gives the edge to the European team. Travelling is always difficult and the fans will be a big part of it: 80–85 per cent are going to be pro-European.

'We're competing on a golf course that is played on their tour so the European players are familiar with the venue. And Monty [European captain Colin Montgomerie] gets to set up the golf course the way he wants to as well. We haven't won on foreign soil since 1993 so it's going to be a challenge.'

Pavin wasn't being defeatist, just realistic. He knew the odds were stacked against him and his men. But there was, nonetheless, a belief that if they could freshen up the team with some eager, determined younger players, they might just have a chance. And who better to look to than the world's number-one amateur: the boy who was making a real name for himself and who was now about to become a pro? Sure, it would be a case of dropping him in at the deep end if he did make the team in September 2010: he would only have been playing on the pro circuit for a year. But if he had a successful twelve months, he might be worth a gamble.

Of course, Rickie himself was aware that the Ryder Cup loomed on the horizon twelve months' hence. And he guessed that there might be a chance, albeit probably a slim one, that he might be invited along if he did well in his first full year. In his favour was the fact that he had been such a success in the Walker Cup – that proved he had it in his armoury to play the team game well. Also, he had heard on the grapevine that Pavin would be looking to 'freshen up' his team with younger talent, should anyone prove worthy. So Rickie knew that the real yardstick for selection would be how he performed over the twelve months; that if he proved he was 'worthy', he stood a chance. If he could hack it on the pro courses, his name would likely come up more and more in conversations as the clock ticked down to the Celtic Manor tournament.

It was a true incentive for Rickie to hit the ground running in his pro career and, a year later, Pavin – who had been named as US skipper for the Ryder Cup in December 2008 – would admit that he had been keeping a close eye on the youngster after his appointment, saying, 'I had a gut feeling about him.'

Rickie was excited that he suddenly had become a pro and was now eligible to play against the big boys and test himself against them. He had gone as far as he could as an amateur – there were no more challenges. He was number one in the world and that was it. He was ready to make the transition; which he needed to do if he was to continue progressing in order to realise his true potential.

Indeed, he remarked, 'It feels like I have completed my amateur career as I wanted to. It was awesome to go out with that Walker Cup win. Ten years from now I want to be the No. 1 player in the world and have a few majors under my belt.' He was confident from the very start; no watered-down ambitions for this guy... it was a case of number one or bust.

Just days after declaring that he had left the amateur field for good, Rickie was able to announce that he had signed a major sponsorship deal. It had been weeks in the making and it was a further sign of just how highly regarded he was in the golf world. He had agreed to a multi-year equipment contract with Titleist, the US brand leader in golf balls, golf clubs and golf accessories. Soon after he would also sign on the dotted line to promote Puma's golf clothing range. Both companies were major players in the world of golf and their determination and urgency to sign up Rickie as soon as he turned pro provided an indication of how highly he was rated after his amateur years – and how he was also deemed to be a potential major champion. Firms like Puma and Titleist were renowned for their hard-nosed business deals; they were not going to plough thousands of pounds into promoting a twenty-year-old youngster unless they were extremely confident he could deliver on the golf course.

The firms believed that Rickie would deliver, that he would become an icon for young golfers and, therefore, increase their profiles, sales markets and profit levels. He would benefit but so would they as Rickie brought a new, younger audience to the sport and, ultimately, to their products. It was a win-win situation for both sides – as Wally Uihlein, chairman and CEO of Acushnet, the parent company of Titleist, explained: 'Rickie is the type of person and player with whom we are proud to be associated,' said Uihlein. 'Although he is only twenty years old, he has already played extensively at the highest level of amateur golf. The experience he gained in college and as a member of the two victorious Walker Cup teams and a Palmer Cup team is immeasurable as he embarks upon his goal to succeed at the highest level of professional golf. Rickie is also among the most likeable young men that I have been around and he will be a great ambassador for the Titleist brand.'

Rickie himself was 'thrilled' at the big break – not many players were offered such a potentially lucrative deal as soon as they turned pro. He said, 'I have played Titleist golf balls and equipment for as long as I can remember. I am ecstatic and appreciative to be able to expand that relationship with Titleist as a professional. I look forward to working with its unmatched Tour Leadership team and taking advantage of the state-of-the-art Titleist Performance Institute which will assist me in achieving my goals.'

As he explained, the breakthrough got him off to a great start in his career. He would have all the top golfing equipment to call upon, plus the publicity garnered by Titleist, as he now embarked on his dream to become the world's number-one player. It was a terrific start and he couldn't wait to get to work.

If there was any debit side to his decision to turn pro, it was that he did have to quit college two years early to do so. He had loved his time at Oklahoma State University and had been contemplating a business major. He may have left by September 2009 but he continued to show his loyalty to the university by wearing its colours and promoting it with its logo when playing in tournaments around the world. Rickie has the OSU logo on his golf bag, wears orange every Sunday and has orange on his irons. He had gone, but no way would he be forgotten at the university. Just as he continued to promote it, so the university was just as proud to put on its website that Rickie had spent two years with them – and that he was one of their most famous students ever.

Reuters were one of many news agencies to comment on his devotion to the OSU as he trotted out for the final day of the 2010 British Open at St Andrews in Scotland:

There was no missing Rickie Fowler at the British Open on Sunday as the American's electrifying golf was matched only by his head-to-toe bright orange outfit … With his hair peeking out from underneath his cap, Fowler was a vision in orange. Baseball cap, shirt, belt, trousers, shoes, even his watch did not escape the visual overload. The world number 37's flowing hair was even tinged with a hint of orange, but his outfit was a tribute to his old school rather than a fashion competition with equally colourful fellow American John Daly, who sported stars and stripes trousers for his final round.

To which Rickie later remarked with a wry grin: 'Not many people wear orange so it's a good way to stand out a bit! I played college golf at Oklahoma State, school colours are orange and black.'

After turning pro, Rickie admitted that he had actually planned to do so even earlier but felt a commitment to his teammates for the 2009 Walker Cup. 'If it wasn't for the Walker Cup, I'd probably be turning earlier,' he told *NewsOK.com*. Once that event was out of the way, he embraced the life of a professional with consummate ease and dedication. He was a golfer who understood the realities: that you were lucky to have God-given talent but that to get to the top and to stay there also required putting in hour after hour of practice and working hard on your game. There was always scope to improve your swings and your putts. You were never done; you couldn't allow complacency to drip into your game or your mental approach if you wanted to be the best.

Even in August 2008, a full thirteen months before joining the pro ranks, he had told *Golfweek* that the time spent practising was key to his development. He admitted that he 'coached himself' although he would occasionally pop in to see Barry McDonnell, the teaching pro who had helped him since he was aged seven, and that, unlike many players, he did not rely on video reruns of shots he had played to perfect them. 'We never used a video camera; Barry's just gone with impact and ball flight,' he said. 'I think that helped in the long run, because I'm not worried about where I need to be in certain parts of my swing or any stuff like that. It's a lot less stressful when you're out there and not hitting the ball well. Barry taught me to flight the ball really well. You have to know how to control your ball.'

He said that he had always been an independent spirit and was disciplined enough to ensure he did work at his game to improve. He never simply thought, 'I've cracked it now, I'll be able to just turn up and win event after event.'

And he also made a point of never cutting back on gym work before going out to practise. Rickie worked out in the gym with a fitness coach to build up the strength in his arms and legs. Only then would he move on to practise his strokes on the golf course. Soon after turning pro, Rickie teamed up with PGA tour fitness coach Chris Noss to improve his strength and flexibility still further. Athletic Golf Training (AGT) revealed exactly how Noss and Rickie worked to get him in top shape for tournaments. On their website, they detailed the routine the duo followed, saying:

> The Rickie Fowler gym workout starts with a few days of plyometrics, a form of exercise that was developed for Olympic athletes. The coach prefers a routine that makes Rickie use all of the muscles that he uses on the course, and hopping and jumping seem to fit his requirements. Dynamic resistance techniques require muscles to stretch and shorten in rapid succession. A positive outcome is the reduction of impact on joints as well as increasing the height an athlete can achieve in a vertical jump with muscular explosiveness.
>
> By the middle of the week, Rickie switches to strength exercises and finishes the week by practising golf functions. Workouts typically last for one hour, with the coach requiring Rickie to perform up to 30 routines every other day and cardio workouts on days in between. The ultimate goal is to provide exercise for all joints, muscles and ligaments that are involved in swinging a club.

When not on the tour circuit, Rickie worked out six days a week. During the week preceding a tournament, he would go for cardio exercises and liked to use his mountain bike when not in the gym, with the overall aim being to 'build endurance for tournament week, and to keep his body moving smoothly'.

The proof of the pudding, as they say, is in the eating or, in Rickie's case, the performances on the green. And his first pro tournament came just days after his announcement that he had left the amateur ranks for good. On 17 September 2009 he teed off in the first round of the Albertson's Boise Open at Hillcrest Country Club in Boise, Idaho. The event was a regular fixture on the Nationwide Tour and was first staged in 1990. The Nationwide Tour season was made up of twenty-nine big-money tournaments, six of which were played away from America. The attraction for the likes of Rickie Fowler in 2009 was clear: the top twenty-five players on the Tour's year-end money list would be rewarded with a PGA Tour card for the following year.

As he teed off at Boise, it was also announced that Rickie would play in the following month's Nationwide Tour's inaugural Soboba Classic at the Country Club at Soboba Springs in San Jacinto. He then summed up this stage of his career with the words: 'I'm just going to try to play as well as I can at these first few events I have lined up.' He was dipping a foot in the water carefully; he knew he had the talent and the drive to shock a few rivals but he needed to acclimatise first. He was no fool; he would have plenty of time to run with the winners. For now, he was the humble guy who listened to advice from his seniors and was always willing to learn from it.

Before teeing off, he had posed happily with the golf bag presented to him by Titleist, who were now his official sponsors. But nerves seemed to get the better of him as he carded 73 and 71 and duly missed the cut by three strokes. His first professional round saw him card three bogeys before a birdie on the par-five sixteenth hole. In the second round he recorded a birdie and an eagle in the first three holes but was unable to build upon them and ended up out of contention at the first hurdle. It had been a disappointing debut but no way did Rickie allow it to knock his confidence. He knew the experience would serve him well and, given the pressures of the day, was just glad to have got his debut out of the way. He would learn from it; he would analyse his faults and then try to put things right in practice sessions.

Always keen to further his golfing education, Rickie stayed on to watch the tournament unfold. It provided him with tips and ideas for the future as veteran Fran Quinn held off the challenge of Blake Adams, who had led until the final round. The message from Quinn's triumph was clear: don't give up, even if it looks as if you are fighting a lost cause. Quinn had stayed strong and eventually proved that it was him, not Adams, who had the steadiest nerve after the pair had tied for the lead on the eighteenth hole.

Rickie left Boise determined to make up for missing the cut in his next event, the PGA's Justin Timberlake Shriners Hospital for Children Open. The event that the former NSync singer had put his name to what was to be held at the TPC at Summerlin in Las Vegas. It was famed as the event in which Tiger Woods notched his first win on the PGA Tour back in 1996. The man who would become the most famous golfer ever shot a sixty-four in the final round to tie with Davis Love III but ended victorious on the first play-off hole.

In 1996 the era of 'The Tiger' was upon us but in 2009 Rickie Fowler couldn't quite match Woods's undoubted brilliance. Having said that, he didn't do that badly either, considering this was his debut on the PGA Tour and only his second outing as a new pro. After the disappointment of missing the cut in Idaho, Rickie now finished tied for seventh in Vegas.

Scotland's Martin Laird emerged as the victor. And just as Rickie had been making a name for himself with his exploits as an amateur, so Laird also entered the record books in Rickie's second pro event. Laird's triumph in a three-man play-off earned him his first PGA Tour win and meant he had become the first Scot to win a PGA Tour event in America since Sandy Lyle had won the 1988 Masters Tournament. Laird also made history by becoming the first Scotsman to win any PGA Tour event since Paul Lawrie had won the British Open a decade earlier.

Rickie congratulated Laird and told friends that it showed you could achieve anything, however long you had to work at it. Obviously, he had no wish to wait until middle age before he won an event but his attitude highlighted his growing maturity. Sure, he was a boy in a rush to reach the very top but he understood it would probably take long hours of practice and some setbacks on the way. But Laird's win proved anything was possible in golf.

Rickie was 'absolutely delighted' with his own seventh-place finish, achieved through four fine rounds in the sixties.

A bonus from that top-ten finish was that it earned him a spot in the next PGA tournament, the Frys.com Open at Grayhawk Golf Club in Scottsdale, Arizona. Things were moving fast; within the space of two events he had laid down a marker suggesting he was certainly one to watch in the world of golf. And his seventh-place finish also earned him $113,700 in prize money. He was finally earning big bucks and on his way to being accepted as a 'proper' pro.

Considering Scottsdale was only his second outing as a pro in a PGA tournament, he did wonderfully well, finishing tied for the runner-up spot with Jamie Lovemark after a surprise collapse by Troy Matteson. However, a three-way play-off ended with a victory for Matteson. The brilliant display by Rickie – achieved with rounds of 65, 64, 69, 64 – also meant his bank balance swelled as he earned another $440,000. It had seemed possible at one point that Rickie might even win the tournament but Matteson managed to pull his game together in the play-off after he had bogeyed the seventeenth and eighteenth holes in regulation time. Matteson birdied the second hole in the play-off to finally emerge victorious.

At one stage Rickie stormed into the lead after notching his fourth hole-in-one. But he was nonetheless 'thrilled' with finishing tied for second. He said, 'I knew I was capable of coming out and competing. But to finish tied for seventh and then tied for first and then losing a play-off – well, it's a pretty quick start!' He also expressed the belief that even being part of the play-off would stand him in good stead. 'I think the more play-offs you're in, the more comfortable you feel. I'm always going to have nerves but maybe next time I'll feel just a little bit more comfortable than I did today.'

Rickie's next stop should have been the Viking Classic but torrential downpours meant that it was rained off, as the course at the Annandale Golf Club in Madison, Mississippi became waterlogged. So it was mid-November before he next teed off, hoping to make his mark at the Children's Miracle Network Classic in Lake Buena Vista, Florida. He finished tied for fortieth after a testing four days, carding rounds of 66, 75, 69 and 72. It was a disappointment: he had hoped to finish high enough to avoid having to attend the PGA Tour qualifying school in December.

Rickie refused to be downbeat. Defiantly, he vowed that he would make it on to the tour. He said, 'I had a great month last month and I will find a way to get out here. I feel like I can play with these guys. I have put up a couple of good finishes. You never know, it could be going to Q-school, it could be a few years of grinding it out trying to get exemptions, but we will find a way to get out here.'

He was as good as his word as he proved himself at the tour school in December 2009, his final round of seventy leaving him tied for fifteenth. Those efforts earned him the key to the door – the much-coveted PGA Tour card for 2010. Now he breathed a big sigh of relief – it meant that he could play in the PGA's main events without having to go through the constant hassle of qualifying. 'Rickie was overjoyed,' a source said. 'This was what he had been working for and now all the hard work and hours spent practising had paid off. He told his friends he would have some time off at Christmas relaxing with his family and then he would spend time getting in shape for the PGA tournaments in the New Year. He was so happy – and so were his family and close friends. He had come a long way in a short time.'

The then world number three, Steve Stricker, spoke for the PGA regulars when asked what he thought of Rickie's progress: 'Nothing but a great addition. I was able to play with him at the U.S. Open when it was in San Diego a couple of years ago. I saw what kind of talent he had at that age. It's pretty cool, to have a young kid with that much talent, and he's a good kid, too. It's nice to see that he got his card.'

A sure sign of just how far the boy from Murrieta, California had come in a short space of time arrived just before he headed off on that well-earned festive vacation. He was chosen to take part in the famous Shark Shootout in Naples, Florida. Rickie was selected by golfing legend Greg Norman for the event and, as the PGA themselves reported, this was indicative of his progress. The official PGA line on the Shootout said, 'Tournament host Greg Norman has completed his annual puzzle of placing a collection of the best players in the world into two-man teams as the 21st annual Shark Shootout returns to Tiburón Golf Club at The Ritz-Carlton Golf Resort in Naples in December.'

There it was in black and white. He had only just turned pro but already Rickie was viewed as one of 'the best players in the world' – and by a guy who should know after a lifetime of tournament wins.

The PGA also paid tribute to Rickie's fast rise in the sport, saying he was '…a 20-year-old with an impressive amateur career. Fowler turned professional this fall and finished in the top 10 in two of the three TOUR events he played during the last four weeks. One of those was a play-off loss in the Frys.com Open. He will be the youngest player in Shootout history to compete.'

Rickie understood the honour bestowed upon him as the youngest player ever in Shootout history. He said, 'I am obviously thrilled to be playing in The Shark Shootout. Greg Norman is one of the most dynamic players in our game's history and it is very exciting to be invited to play in an event that he hosts. In addition, I have learned we will be helping raise awareness and funds for CureSearch. It will be a pleasure for me to assist this organisation and the tournament as they both seek ways to benefit the lives of children not as fortunate as me.'

Helping those less fortunate than himself would become a regular feature of Rickie's rise, leading to him eventually forming his own charitable foundation. He was a young man fully aware of the privileges bestowed upon him as a new sporting icon and he had always been altruistic in nature. In this instance, the CureSearch National Childhood Cancer Foundation and other worthy charities would benefit.

And Greg Norman himself paid tribute to Rickie and the others who were giving their time to help out. Norman said:

When I was putting the final pieces together, I realised what a great group of players we have this year. Overall, these players are talented professionals who are generous both on and off the golf course, not to mention fun to be around. I am confident fans and our television audience will enjoy the competition and the entertainment.

Of course, at the end of the day, they all will be trying to win. When you factor in that 12 PGA TOUR tournament titles this year alone have been won by this group and the fact that 12 of them are highly ranked in the world, the spirit of competition will be intense.

Rickie was paired with Tour regular Chris DiMarco and the organisers summed up their attributes in this way: 'DiMarco is a three-time TOUR winner, has finished second in two major championships since 2005 and will provide experience for Fowler, who's playing in his first Shark Shootout. Fowler is certainly one of the hottest players coming into the week, with two top-10 finishes in three starts in the last month. The colourful Fowler, age 20, is the youngest player in Shootout history.'

Speaking at the Shootout, Rickie said he was delighted that Puma had done a deal with him to have their name advertised on his hats and shirts. 'Puma was just an awesome fit with kind of the edgy, non-traditional golf style. And that kind of sums up who I am. I'm not the traditional golfer. I'm not in the khakis and white shirt or anything all of the time.'

He admitted that he admired the unique-style fashion of fellow Shootout golfer Ian Poulter, saying, 'I'm sure you'll be able to pick the two of us out at times with what we might wear. Puma are coming out with some funky styles. They've got their own look, which is nice. I think they make good product[s]. When you're associated with one of the brands like that, you're going to be noticed on the golf course, which is good.'

But he also made it clear that his main ambition was to be renowned for his golf, rather than the snazzy gear he might wear around the courses. He said, 'I'd definitely like to see myself going into next year and giving myself opportunities to win. I don't see any reason why I shouldn't be at the top of the leader boards if I play well. It would be nice if Chris and I were holding up the trophy on Sunday.'

But it was not to be – it was a tournament too soon for the youngster, as Steve Stricker and Jerry Kelly won by a stroke, carding a final round fifty-nine to finish thirteen-under-par. Kenny Perry and J.B. Holmes had led for most of the day, only to fluff their lines at the end of the event. 'It's another feather in our cap,' said Stricker. 'It was a lot of fun. We came here to have fun and to play well at the same time, and we did that.'

Rickie and DiMarco finished seventh at twenty-under-par with a final round of sixty-two. It was a credible result in a high-class field and Rickie could afford to smile as he prepared for the final round. It was his twenty-first birthday and the crowd burst into an impromptu chorus of 'Happy Birthday'! He was a player already well loved on the circuit by his fellow pros and the fans and he was just twenty-one and just turned pro. As Rickie Fowler headed off for that well-earned Christmas break, he could reflect upon a great year and make plans for a great future. The boy was on his way to golfing superstardom.

CHAPTER THREE

I'M MY OWN MAN

Rickie enjoyed himself during the festive season of 2009 and celebrated the New Year of 2010 with his family and friends. But by 2 January he was back in 'business mode', preparing for the first tournaments of the year, the Sony Open in Honolulu and the Bob Hope Classic in La Quinta, California. As he is teetotal, there was no need to detox or sweat off the festive excesses: he was also not one to indulge in too much calorific food. And, as always, he was eager to get back on the golf course.

He spent time perfecting his game and, after saying goodbye to his parents, was in a confident mood as he embarked upon the journey to Honolulu for the Sony Open. He was physically in good condition and mentally and emotionally geed up. After all, he had waited for this moment for many years – the dawn of his first full season on the PGA Tour circuit – and now it was here and Rickie was ready to roll.

Before the event, he was asked by the press pack how he felt when fellow pros and pundits said he was a champion in the making. He answered:

It's definitely cool that people are out there talking about me like that. But I look at it as people are saying there's that possibility. I'm just looking forward to this full year. Goal-wise I'd like to obviously keep my card. My own expectations are just to get the most that I can out of every week because you can be on top of the game one week and then you're struggling the next.

I expect myself to play well, whether that's winning a few events or maybe some top-10s here and there. I'll just go out and keep doing what I've been doing and just keep playing my game. I really don't try and worry much about what people are saying or writing about me.

And when asked about his colourful image and personality, he stressed once again that he would be his own man, whatever others might think of him. He laughed when it was suggested to him – yet again – that he was the Leonardo DiCaprio of golf; that his unorthodox looks and laid-back style made him a doppelganger for the movie heartthrob. Rickie said, 'Sometimes people give me a hard time about the hair, the hats are too big, they're flopping over my ears, stuff like that. But it's what I'm doing. It's kind of my own style.

'I'm not exactly the traditional golfer. I didn't grow up at a country club. Just a kid that grew up at a driving range. I used to hit buckets of balls.'

Golf blogger Larry Fein perceptively also zoomed in on the DiCaprio line and how Fowler was offbeat but a potential champion too. Fein said:

Leonardo DiCaprio look-a-like Rickie Fowler is starting his first full season [of] the PGA Tour this week at the Sony Open in Hawaii … Fowler has been a standout at every level in golf. From the junior golf ranks to high school to two All-American years at Oklahoma State to two Walker Cups. Plus, he's already had some success in the pro ranks, losing in play-offs in a Nationwide Tour and PGA Tour event last year, then getting through the final stage of Q School to earn his PGA Tour card. So is he destined to save the PGA Tour in 2010 and become the next Tiger Woods? Ya never know.

Rickie told a press conference held before the Bob Hope Classic how excited he was about taking part in his first full season on the PGA circuit. He said, 'I'm just looking forward to this full year. It's nice to start it over here in Hawaii. Kind of like an extended vacation. Then to get to go back near home and play a few events, kind of a little bit of a slower start to the schedule for me, to be here in Hawaii, then sometime around home to kind of relax.'

He also admitted that now and again he still liked to ride

his motorbike to relax; that although he could no longer compete in motocross, he still enjoyed the freedom and exhilaration of riding.

> I started riding [motocross] and playing golf about the same time – I had done both since I was three. I was always more into golf. I liked the individual aspect, kind of doing things on my own. It's the same way with riding, too. But there was something about golf that just drew me in a little bit more. I still ride every once in a while, hop on the bike to go out and have a little bit of free time, let loose a bit. I think the riding has helped me a bit with golf. It's something I'll never give up.

Unfortunately, things would not go to plan in Honolulu, as Rickie failed to make the cut at the Sony Open and ended up outside the prize money with two rounds of seventy-five and seventy-two. But he had played and his experience of playing with the big boys was adding up – the field had included such golfing luminaries as defending champion Zach Johnson, Ernie Els, Vijay Singh, Retief Goosen, Angel Cabrera and John Daly.

There was little time to mope and Rickie had never been one for massive inquests after a tournament. He believed in looking forward, not backwards and flew back to the US mainland for a couple of days' rest and recuperation. Then, less than a fortnight later, he was making the 400-km trip from his Vegas home to La Quinta, California for the Bob Hope

Classic. He ended up with a final score of 294, consisting of four rounds of 74, 70, 75 and 75. Winner of the event was fellow American Bill Haas and it was extra special for the twenty-seven-year-old as it was Haas's maiden victory on the PGA Tour.

Rickie applauded Haas along with the other pros at the post-tournament award-presentation ceremony. He saw once again that with dedication and hard work it was possible to reach the peak of the golfing summit: Haas had just proved that, as he had previously never finished higher than third. Yet here he was lifting the trophy at the first PGA event of 2010.

And Haas had been forced to overcome a serious bout of nerves to emerge triumphant – something Rickie never had a problem with. Haas admitted as much afterwards, when he told the crowd, 'This feels unbelievable. I was so nervous coming down the stretch. I still don't know how I hit the shot on eighteen – my hands were shaking. I told my caddie on the last hole, "I am as nervous as hell." And he said, "Well, that's a good thing."'

Later, Rickie said he was disappointed with his own showing. For the second consecutive tournament he had missed the cut and he conceded that his final round of seventy-five had been 'terrible' and that 'my swing didn't feel so good so I am going to work on that.' He had expected to do so much better but was mature enough to accept that he wouldn't always be able to live up to expectations: that golf, like any major sport, could end up taking you by surprise on occasions and leave you feeling deflated. Rickie knew that when that occasionally happened, he had to just put it down to being 'one of those days', not get too wound up by it and move forward as quickly as possible to the next challenge.

If you could also pinpoint just where you had gone wrong, you could also work thoroughly on that aspect of your game to put things right. In this case, he would concentrate all his efforts on getting his swing back in shape before his next appointment. Rickie Fowler was a rookie pro with a divine talent whose time would come – he would win a major one day. The only debatable part of the equation was whether it would be sooner rather than later.

For now, Rickie was glad to get the experience of different events under his belt. He had struggled in the New Year sunshine in Honolulu and La Quinta but his next adventure in the sun would bring a welcome boost to his fledgling career as a pro on the competitive PGA circuit. In the Farmers Insurance Open at Torrey Pines, San Diego, Rickie basked in the sunshine and the outcome as he finished tied for fifth with an 11-under-par total of 277. His sponsors, Puma, had set the scene for him before he teed off, telling golf fans to look out for him as he played at a venue just over an hour away from his hometown of Murrieta, and trumpeting:

Puma golfer, Rickie Fowler, is making his much anticipated season debut this week at The Farmers Insurance Open at Torrey Pines in La Jolla, CA. The Southern California native has good vibes at the famed

Torrey Pines golf courses, having made the cut as an amateur in the 2008 U.S. Open and having finished fifth at last year's Farmers. Rickie is sure to have large galleries rooting him on this week as he grew up an hour away in Murrieta, CA.

Having finished the 2010 season with three top 5 finishes in the Fall Series of the PGA Tour schedule, many golf insiders are predicting a breakthrough win for Rickie. Best of luck to you this week Rickie! Let's get this party started…

Rickie's four rounds consisted of a brilliant opening card of sixty-seven and then a hat-trick of seventies. The performance also earned him prize money of $186,163 – no wonder he was pictured smiling at the end of his four days' work!

Rickie was also just two shots adrift of winner Ben Crane: it had been a fine display by the youngster that had seen him tie for fifth with the likes of Ernie Els. At the post-event press conference Rickie admitted that he was 'delighted' and summed up his final-round performance in this way: 'I got off to a good start, good lag putts to save some pars and finally made a good birdie on 4. I played fairly solid from there and just made one rough swing on seventeen that cost me a couple. But I came back with a birdie, two-under for the day. I got a top-ten finish and it's a nice way to start the year.'

Rickie explained that the result had been good for his confidence, as he now had a finish to back up his belief that he could make an impact on the tour. He had finished a creditable fifth and was now keen to build upon that foundation and go on to win an event. As ever, he was confident of himself and his ability.

That self-belief would pay dividends at the end of February 2010 as Rickie chalked up his joint best result ever. He finished runner-up in the Waste Management Phoenix Open in Scottsdale, Arizona, just a few months after ending up tied for the same spot at the Frys.com Open. But the result in Arizona was the big breakthrough he had been aiming for in his first full season as a pro: it sent a message to his rivals, both young and old, that he had arrived and that he really did mean business. He was not interested in simply finishing mid-leader board at events and collecting a tidy amount of cash. No, he wanted to finish top of the leader board and the cash would look after itself. Rickie Fowler was more interested in the glory and entering the history books than the potential financial rewards during that 2010 debut season.

The Phoenix success meant that he could breathe easily over his PGA card. It propelled him to the top of the rookie rankings and ensured he would keep his Tour card for the following season. It was only February, yet he had managed to ease the pressure considerably. He could now play his golf without constantly looking over his shoulder to see if he was doing enough to keep the coveted card. Rickie said, 'I think it basically gives me my card back, which was one of my goals going into the year, and I took care of that pretty quick, which is kind of a relief. I get to just go play golf now.

It moves me up in the rankings with the reshuffle, so a lot of good things have happened this week.'

Rickie lost out for the $1 million first prize to his friend and former Oklahoma State star Hunter Mahan. Rickie carded rounds of 65, 67, 69 and 68 to finish with a 15-under par total of 269 – and a purse of $648,000. He was particularly pleased with his first-round sixty-five, which began with six birdies and no bogeys. Rickie said, 'It was nice. We were cruising along and I told my caddie, "Let's see if we can get through the turn bogey-free." I started off well with six birdies on the front nine and had a few good birdies toward the end.'

He was also happy with his final round, which ensured the runner-up spot – a bogey-free three-under-par sixty-eight with birdies on the fifth, thirteenth and fourteenth holes. Rickie said, 'I played solid, bogey-free, gave myself a few looks there at the end. Ultimately, what I wanted was to have a chance coming down the last few holes. That's what I did.' And he admitted that it was less painful to lose to Mahan given that he was a fellow student at Oklahoma State. 'I've spent a bit of time with him. I saw him in Stillwater a little bit when I was there at school, and I got to know him a bit more being out here. It's good to see him win, and it's always a little bit better to lose to a Cowboy!'

Rickie was making progress and within another four months would have secured his third runner-up spot on the tour – and he was only twenty-one. That success came at the renowned Memorial Tournament in Dublin, Ohio.

Cameron Morfit, of *Golf* magazine, brilliantly summed up what it meant for Rickie's place in the golfing hierarchy after he shot a fine second-round sixty-six: 'The future of golf wore lime sherbet Friday. Or maybe it was sea foam, or mint, or hospital green. While everyone else was clucking over his outfit, Rickie Fowler, 21, painted the scoreboard red, making an eagle and four birdies for a second-round 66 that put him at 13 under par and tied the 36-hole scoring record at the Memorial.'

Not bad for a twenty-one-year-old rookie! He was on target for a top-five finish and the fact that he had equalled the course-scoring record was some achievement. Rickie was beginning to do what he had set out to do: he was now in the record books for his golfing brilliance, making Memorial history with that wonder round.

Justin Rose beat him to the winner's spot at the Memorial to achieve his first win on the PGA Tour, so records were being set all around on the famous Ohio course. Rickie held his hands up and said he had never imagined he would have carded a sixty-five in the first round, continuing, 'I didn't see myself shooting 65 on it today. I saw this as being a pretty tough course, had to drive it well. The greens are pretty tricky so I was pretty pleased to score 65 in the first round of the tournament.'

And after he secured second spot on the final day, he told the assembled press pack that he had enjoyed an 'awesome' time. He said, 'It was an awesome week. Justin [Rose] put up a great round today, so got to give it up to him. And I now look forward to hopefully being in contention a little bit more often. I felt really comfortable out there.

'The game's felt great all week. I finally had some success driving the ball, the irons have been good, my short game was good and I made some putts.'

He was asked to describe his personality as a golfer while playing a round and answered: 'I am quick, pretty laid-back and easy-going.' And did he accept he was one of a 'new generation' of young golfers making their mark? 'I think so. A lot of the guys are still pretty young with McIlroy, Ryo [Ishikawa] and Ricky Barnes in that category. Justin Rose is also still in that category. I think a lot of us are just getting started and have a long way to go.'

Rickie and the so-called golfing 'Brat Pack' may have been just getting started – but they were sure pulling out all the stops and making their presence felt. Rickie had shown the way forward with his self-belief, impressive strokes on the golf course and fearless drives and putts. Along with the UK's Rory McIlroy, he was marking himself out as one of the two best kids among the new kids on the block.

And as the second part of the season took hold, Rickie would make an argument for being the best as he won the Rookie of the Year award for 2010 to add to his impressive finishes in his debut season as a pro. The best was clearly yet to come for the nattily dressed, confident young man from southern California.

CHAPTER FOUR

EASY RYDER

Rickie was making waves in the tough world of pro golf. His runner-up finish in the Memorial not only equalled his best performance and made him that much richer, it also propelled him into the top fifty in the world rankings. He was making a name for himself and earning the respect of his fellow pros. They recognised talent when they saw it and, unlike in some other sports, were decent people who applauded youthful vigour and the emergence of new stars. Nick Faldo was impressed by Rickie's 'youthful confidence' and Justin Rose praised him for his determination and efforts in the Memorial.

Rickie was ranked number thirty-two in the world after the event at Muirfield Village and his confidence was soaring. But he then experienced a setback when he failed to qualify for the US Open. But at least he was in good company – Justin

Rose, who had beat him to the top spot at the Memorial, also didn't do well enough to qualify. 'This is my third week in a row playing,' Rickie said by way of explanation. 'Being in contention definitely wears you out quite a bit. Now I'm looking forward to some time off. It would have been nice to be playing in the Open, but it happens.'

Three months later Rickie was refreshed and celebrating some wonderful news. He was one of the four picks selected by America captain Corey Pavin for the Ryder Cup. It was a tremendous boost to his confidence and a reflection of just how far he truly had come in such a short space of time. Rickie joined his teammates at a special pre-tournament press briefing at the New York Stock Exchange at the start of September 2010. And he wasted no time in admitting that he was indebted to Pavin for giving him his big chance. Rickie said he had found it difficult to sleep the night before and explained just what it meant to him, saying, 'I have to thank Corey for selecting me. This is a pretty special opportunity. The last time I played overseas on a team event was for the Walker Cup [in which he excelled]. So I hope to take some of the knowledge I learned there to help the team. I can bring some youth to the team and hopefully get the guys pumped up.'

The Press Association (PA) had revealed in the previous July just how keen Rickie had become to win a place in the US Ryder Cup team. He told *PA Sport* that the tournament was far from the front of his mind and planning when he first turned pro but that, after his fine performances on the

PGA Tour, he had got a taste for playing in high-pressure tournaments against the best golfers in the world and that making it into the American team would mean a lot to him. He admitted to the PA in July 2010, 'Now it's one of my main goals, but for the moment I'm just enjoying playing against the best players in the world.'

And by making it into the team, Rickie wrote another page in golf's history books by becoming the first player since Tiger Woods to advance straight from the Walker Cup to the Ryder Cup.

Some pundits were 'surprised' that Pavin had chosen Rickie. They argued that he was too young and would not be able to withstand the attendant pressures that came with playing in one of golf's premier events. The *Daily Mail* led the way in chronicling how surprisingly 'left field' Pavin's choice of Rickie had been, saying:

For his most important announcement as US Ryder Cup captain, Corey Pavin chose a place as far removed from the highly charged environment of Celtic Manor imaginable.

In the sedate splendour of the New York Stock Exchange's oak-panelled Main Dining Hall, 21-year-old Rickie Fowler emerged from left field as the most ambitious selection among his four personal picks. There was little doubt that he would confirm Tiger Woods' participation, or that he would go with the reliability of Stewart Cink and Zach Johnson, but thrusting in the blond Californian is a bold move.

South Wales in 22 days' time will serve up an atmosphere rather different to that created on Monday by waiters in aprons with their bone china and silver sets. Pavin believes that, as the youngest of five rookies in his 12-man team, Fowler can handle it. The idea is for him to provide the youthful exuberance that Anthony Kim did last time out for the Americans, and that Rory McIlroy will, hopefully, counter-balance for Europe this time.

Pavin was asked just why he had chosen the youngster as one of his four picks for Team USA. He said, 'It just came down to feelings. I had a gut feeling about Rickie. He has a very good Walker Cup record and he is a very good player.' It was also put to Pavin whether Rickie would be able to cope with the pressure, how highly charged the atmosphere at the event in Wales could be. The skipper said he had no worries on that count: 'I think he can handle it and that's why I picked him. He's a very mature young man and had experience of international play [in the Walker Cup]. He's a very solid player and he has got a very steady head on his shoulders.'

At the tender age of twenty-one years and nine months when the event teed off, Rickie ensured his entry into the record books yet again – this time as the youngest player. It would be the thirty-eighth time the event had taken place and the seventeenth occasion when it would be held in the UK, albeit the first time in Wales. The tournament was to take place on a brand-new course at the Celtic Manor Resort in

Newport, which had been specially made for the Ryder Cup
– the so-called Twenty Ten course. The organisers issued a
statement for public consumption about the course and how
they hoped the tournament would pan out. It read:

> Opened in July 2007, the course combines nine
> spectacular new holes designed by European Golf
> Design with nine holes from the original Robert
> Trent Jones Jnr-designed Wentwood Hills golf course
> which have been extensively remodelled. The new
> course measures 7,493 yards from the back tees with
> a par of 71.
>
> The brief was to create a golf course that could deal
> with the particular requirements of hosting a Ryder Cup
> in addition to challenging the world's greatest players in
> Tournament competition. Close coordination between
> European Golf Design and The European Tour Staging
> Department ensured that the design catered for all the
> elements needed to stage a major sports event including
> creating areas for tented villages, building dedicated
> platforms for hospitality units, incorporating space for
> all the media and television requirements, providing
> good spectator viewing points and ensuring practical
> and safe public access.
>
> Vast platforms for corporate hospitality were
> constructed running virtually the entire length of
> the final three holes, while the slopes below these
> platforms offer superb viewing for thousands of

spectators not only of these holes, but across the whole of the golf course.

Ross McMurray of European Golf Design said:

It has been a great privilege to play a part in the development of the Twenty Ten Course at Celtic Manor Resort and to have the opportunity to create a golf course that is not only capable of challenging the world's greatest players but can also deal with all the requirements of staging a Ryder Cup. It has also been an interesting exercise to successfully balance the various requirements of engineers, archaeologists, ecologists and The European Tour Staging Department with the need to create a golf course that will host both The Celtic Manor Wales Open and The Ryder Cup – as well as provide a high quality golfing destination for visitors to the resort. It was a real team effort from the start and I would like to thank all those who have been involved in this hugely exciting project.

Certainly Rickie was excited and more nervous than normal when he arrived in Newport, Wales, for the beginning of the tournament on 1 October 2010. But the Ryder Cup organisers offered Rickie a timely boost by describing him in these glowing terms: 'Most everyone agrees that Fowler, arguably the most surprising of Corey Pavin's four captain's picks, will find victory on the PGA Tour soon. Until then the rookie can take solace in his making 16 of 21 cuts, two second-place finishes, five top tens and more than $2.3 million in earnings.'

But Rickie would not get off to a dream start in his debut – a foursomes match with experienced partner Jim Furyk. He made a couple of mistakes, including forfeiting a hole after taking a free drop from mud with a different ball. That meant the duo were two down after only four holes and it dramatically increased the pressure they were now under. It was then to Rickie's credit that he calmed himself down and delivered the goods in brilliant fashion. It was Rickie who putted the last hole for a birdie to halve the match. Afterwards, he was typically honest in his assessment of his performance, saying, 'It was awesome to get a look at a putt to halve the match on the last hole. On hole four I basically dropped the wrong ball. After being down for most of the match and coming into the last hole, it was nice to get a couple of good shots.' At the end of the day, the Americans appeared in command, going in with a 6–4 lead, which meant they needed only eight of the remaining eighteen points to lift the trophy.

It was not to be: the Americans would lose out by the cruellest of margins – just one point. In the Session Three morning 'fourballs' Rickie and Phil Mickelson would lose 2/1 to Ian Poulter and Martin Kaymer. But Rickie would be the hero for the Americans on the final day of the competition, displaying his remarkable talent and self-control as he did his best to help his teammates retain the Ryder trophy. From a seemingly hopeless position, he managed to halve his singles match against Italian ace Edoardo Molinari. Rickie had got off to a disastrous start as he struggled to double-bogey the first hole. But he swiftly showed his resilience by holing out for a birdie and winning the second hole in four. Molinari retook the initiative and looked set for victory with four holes remaining. Yet, somehow, Rickie found an extra layer of inner resolve to birdie those last four holes for that unexpected half. Molinari looked demoralised and deflated: Rickie looked triumphant as he accepted the pats on the back from his impressed teammates.

The Ryder Cup organisers were similarly impressed when they issued their summary of the match, even describing Rickie's late fight-back as 'miraculous'. They added:

Molinari won the opening hole with a par after a great up and down from the right greenside bunker to take a 1-up lead. Molinari conceded the second hole to Fowler after struggling with a chip shot in front of the green to bring the match back to all square. Molinari recaptured the lead by making an 8-foot birdie on No. 3 to get back to 1-up. Fowler's birdie from 10 feet on No. 5 squared the match. Molinari holed a 25-foot birdie putt at the eighth hole to go 1-up. A 5-foot birdie putt by Molinari on No. 10 allowed him to extend his lead to 2-up. At the par-5 11th, Molinari went 3-up after making a 12-foot birdie putt. Molinari continues to pour it on Fowler. After a great approach on No.

12, Molinari gets another birdie and takes a 4-up lead. Fowler won the 13th hole with a par to cut his deficit to 3-down. After Molinari missed a par putt on the 16th hole, he conceded a birdie putt to Fowler who went 2-down with two to play. Fowler nailed a clutch 12-foot birdie putt on No. 17 to go 1-down with one to play. Miraculously, Fowler holed a 15-foot birdie putt on the final hole to fight back from 4-down and earn a halve.

Typically, Rickie refused to make a big deal of his exploits, almost portraying them as a matter of good fortune, or luck, rather than golfing genius. He said, 'It was a position where it was nothing to lose and I had to go for it. Edoardo played great all day. He hit a lot of great shots and forced me to make some putts at the end. On the final putt, I just picked out a spot and told myself to just hit a good putt – and what happened would happen. I hit a good one and it went right in the middle.'

Rickie may have been humble and keen to play down his remarkable work but his teammates were just as keen to make a fuss about what he had achieved. Captain Pavin summed up the general feeling in the American camp when he said:

Rickie will play in many more Ryder Cups. He's a great kid and he's going to be out here a long time. He played well and, as a captain's pick, I thought he would.

That is why I picked him. It's very special to play in Ryder Cups – it's a very strong emotional week. But I think Rickie is a player who can handle that. He gave an incredible performance to halve that singles match. The character he showed and the way he hung in there and then coming back and birdieing the last four holes. It's something he'll remember for the rest of his life and he'll be able to mature and grow as a person.

And *golfday.co.uk* – the experts in golfing trips and tips – were quick to praise Rickie for his technical skill and determination in the tournament, saying: 'The 2010 Ryder Cup was compelling viewing. On singles Sunday there was many impressive performances. Ian Poulter was superb and Graeme McDowell held his nerve under intense pressure. Rickie Fowler displayed fantastic composure to birdie the last 3 holes and keep the USA in the Ryder Cup.'

Urging their readers to watch a video of Rickie's work in the singles match, the golfday experts pointed out how competent he had been with his balance and how calm and still he remained as he waited for the ball to drop on the final holes when he had 'must make' putts. They also heaped praise on the youngster for his 'tremendous confidence' in achieving three straight birdies during the 'pressure-cooker' atmosphere of those last holes.

Rickie was understandably visibly emotional when he spoke about how the tournament had gone and how he had enjoyed it. He said, 'It's been an awesome week for me. At twenty-one, playing [the] Walker Cup last year and to come and play the Ryder Cup this year. It's been pretty cool to be on a team with all these guys. We are all very close. We've got to know each other on a personal level and to know each other's games better. I want to thank Corey for giving me the opportunity to be here. It's been a great week for me.'

Indeed, it had been. Rickie and his teammates were naturally disappointed to have lost the trophy to their European rivals but at least they could hold their heads high and say they had done their best. 'It was a blow to our pride to lose but the narrowness of the defeat meant we could leave Newport with dignity,' a US press officer said on the radio to TalkSport. 'It wasn't as if we were thrashed or anything like that; we were genuinely unlucky and the weather didn't help. They were tough conditions out there with the rain and the wind but we almost came through. We just fell short, it was no disgrace when we were competing away from home and against a tough group of rivals who had home advantage and who were more used to the conditions than us.'

And of Rickie? The press officer went on:

Look, he was the rookie of the team and he did a damned fine job of it in his singles match. OK, he messed up initially but then the way he came back to halve it deserves a lot of praise. His teammates really appreciated him and were talking about he could become a real star if he fulfilled his talent. Everyone in the US team was in agreement that Rickie would one day win a major as he had the talent, the determination and time on his side. He was only 21 yet at times had played as if he were a veteran in this Ryder Cup. He definitely did not seem out of his depth, if anything he overshadowed some of his older, more illustrious teammates like Phil Mickelson. This was a boy who was surely going to have a fantastic career ahead of him.

The Associated Press (AP) succinctly summed up the outcome of the tournament, saying:

> The Europeans won 14½ to 13½ to reclaim the cup won by the Americans at Valhalla two years ago. This was the closest Ryder Cup since 1999, when the Americans rallied from a 10–6 deficit at Brookline for a one-point win.
>
> The youngest American, 21-year-old Rickie Fowler, gave the visiting team hope of pulling off an improbable comeback when he won the final three holes to halve his match with Edoardo Molinari. Fowler rolled in a 15-foot birdie putt at the 17th to extend the match, then made an 18-footer at the final hole to stun the Italian.

Rickie had provided hope, but he couldn't win it by himself. He was the new kid on the block and the seasoned campaigners needed to raise their game if the US were to nick the result. Ultimately, they did just that but the Europeans just had the edge to claim victory. But for Rickie, there was joy mixed in with his own disappointment. Sure, he would have liked to have helped retain the trophy but at least he had taken part and had let no one down. He had surprised some people with his talent and had become a world-renowned name in golf after his exploits in his singles match.

For Rickie Fowler, the path to legendary status in the sport had now well and truly opened up. Less than a year after turning pro, he had made headlines across the world with his deeds at the Celtic Manor Resort. For Rickie Fowler, the times where he could walk down the street without being noticed had gone. He had made his mark and would now be treated like a celebrity. The legend of the boy from small-town California was taking shape – and there would be more triumphs than setbacks as he developed as a golfer with great talent and a most engaging, generous personality.

CHAPTER FIVE

ROOKIE OF
THE YEAR

That exciting journey to Britain as part of the American Ryder Cup team would prove to be one of the highlights of 2010 for Rickie. He had shown himself capable of living with golf's big beasts and that he had the mettle and talent to compete with the very best. But that tournament wasn't the final highlight of his first year as a pro, for in December he was voted Rookie of the Year too. The honour is part of the PGA's annual awards. The winner is chosen by the players, so it is extra special for the recipient. Rickie was 'absolutely delighted' to have been honoured by his fellow pros on the circuit and said he fully understood that the hard part was to now keep up the high-standard level of his golf.

His clothing sponsors Puma were quick to congratulate him – and no doubt just as quick to give themselves a pat on the back for having the nous to tie him up to a long-term deal! – saying, 'We are very pleased to announce that our very own Puma golfer, Rickie Fowler, has won Rookie of the Year! Congrats to Rickie for a very successful year on tour ... Rickie was also selected for the Ryder Cup Team USA, making him the first rookie to ever be chosen to the squad. Job well done Rickie! Cheers to a great season on tour and best of luck in 2011.'

Inevitably, his gear sponsors, Titleist, also insisted on getting in on the act, adding their own message of congratulations:

Titleist brand ambassador Rickie Fowler was named PGA Tour Rookie of the Year over the weekend, capping a tremendous season for the 21-year-old that included a lot of time spent on leader boards, airplanes, television screens and Twitter. He also happened to sign a few autographs and provide one of the more dramatic Ryder Cup moments in recent memory. Fowler, who celebrates his 22nd birthday Dec. 13, currently sits at No. 25 in the Official World Golf Ranking, after beginning the season at the Sony Open in Hawaii at No. 249.

'We're off to a good start,' said Fowler, 'and hopefully we can keep that going.' In 28 official starts this season, Fowler totalled seven top-10s, including runner-up finishes at the Waste Management Phoenix Open and the Memorial Tournament, and had the highest rookie finishes on both the PGA Tour money list (22nd) and the FedEx Cup standings (32nd). 'Shot of the year would have been the putt on 18 at the Ryder Cup,'

Rickie told Team Titleist via text message Monday. 'Putt on 17 (12-footer for birdie) is in there also.'

Once again, Rickie's achievement landed him a page in golf's record books as he became the youngest player to receive the coveted award since a twenty-year-old Tiger Woods did so in 1996.

'Rickie made an immediate splash on the Tour this year and is one of the many rising young stars that look to challenge players such as Jim Furyk in the coming years,' PGA Tour Commissioner Tim Finchem said, explaining exactly why the youngster had deserved to win the award.

USA Today made the important point that Rickie is a much deeper and wiser person than the cartoon image of him as a long-haired rebel would suggest; that his golfing exploits in his first season as a pro and the Rookie of the Year award proved that to be the case: 'Fowler is more than a mop of hair under an oversized golf cap on top of a colorful eclectic wardrobe that features a head-to-toe orange pumpkin get-up for final rounds … Fowler notched seven top-10s on Tour (including runner-up finishes in Phoenix and the Memorial), won $2.8 million, was a captain's pick for the Ryder Cup and was named Rookie of the Year.'

But not everyone was delighted that Rickie had scooped the coveted award. There was an element in the press pack and among the inner golf fraternity that argued – and with some vehemence – that the award should have gone to Rory McIlroy. This would be the first time that Rickie and Rory would be judged head to head but it would certainly not be the last. In effect, this incident represented the firing of the opening shots in a battle between the two that would most likely continue well into the future; quite possibly until one or both of them retired from the game they both loved. These were the opening shots in a battle line that represented on the one hand the glowing youth and pride of the United Kingdom (in the case of Rory) and a similar golden boy for America. It represented also a changing of the guard: the end of an era dominated by Tiger Woods on one side and the likes of Colin Montgomerie on the other. Out with the old, in with the new.

Both Rickie and Rory represented a youthful, shiny, refreshing exuberance when compared with the shame and disgrace suffered by Tiger Woods in his downfall. It was the glint of a new, brave, bright world illuminated on both sides of the Atlantic by Rickie and Rory. It suddenly opened up to a new younger audience as Rickie and Rory battled cleanly for supremacy.

You were either with Rickie, or you were with Rory. Both youngsters drew considerable loyalty and commitment to their cause and supporters of both believed their man was the best and would be the one who would ultimately triumph.

Of course, the duo had already clashed as amateurs. In 2007, as we have noted elsewhere, Rickie played a key role in the USA's Walker Cup victory, beating Rory in team play in the Northern Irishman's homeland at Royal County Down.

Rickie's pal Jonathan Moore had sealed victory for the States by one point as he holed his four-foot eagle putt on the final hole of his match.

Then Rory had gained his revenge in their embryonic days in the pro world as he helped Europe defeat America in the 2010 Ryder Cup. If we were keeping score, that would have meant that Rory had levelled at 1–1 – although Rickie still managed to steal headlines with those brilliant four birdies in his last four holes to halve his singles match against Edoardo Molinari.

Now Rickie had taken a 2–1 lead, forging ahead once again as he was named Rookie of the Year. But the protests against the decision threatened to overshadow his great feat. There had been four names put forward for the honour: Rickie, Rory, Derek Lamely and Alex Prugh. The *Golf Channel* summed up the feeling that it would be Rory who would triumph, saying, 'Four players are on the ballot for Rookie of the Year, and while it would seem to be an easy choice – Rory McIlroy winning at Quail Hollow and finishing in the top three of two Majors – it will be interesting to see how the membership regards his status as a rookie, and his decision not to join the tour next year. The other candidates are Rickie Fowler (No. 22 on money list, Ryder Cup team), Puerto Rico winner Derek Lamely and Alex Prugh.'

Rory had, indeed, had a fine season and the suggestion that he might lose out because he had decided to 'snub' the PGA Tour for the following year resonated with many pundits who declared themselves to be in his corner. The website

SB Nation made the point that, on paper at least, Rory had enjoyed a more successful season:

> Rickie Fowler has been named the PGA Tour Rookie of the Year, the youngest player to receive ROY honors since Tigers Woods won the award in 1996. But Fowler, whose hair would make any Justin Beiber fan melt, took the title amid controversy as Northern Ireland's Rory McIlroy finished second in voting. Although Fowler had an excellent first full season, with two runner-up finishes, seven top-10 finishes and rising to No. 25 in the Official World Golf Rankings after starting the season ranked No. 249, Fowler failed to win a tournament unlike fellow rookie McIlroy. McIlroy, who won at Quail Hallow this year, an elite tournament with a stacked field, also added five top-10 finishes to his first year résumé, including finishing third in the year's final two majors. Both players made the Ryder Cup teams this year as well, however McIlroy's European team topped the Americans.

Rory's friend and golfing ally from England, Lee Westwood, led the voices of disapproval on his Twitter page. Westwood's opinion carried some considerable weight given that he was, at that time, world number one. Westwood said:

> Sorry 140 letters is not going to be enough for this rant! Just seen Ricky Fowler has been given rookie of the

year! Yes he's had a good year but rory mcilroy 3rd in 2 majors and an absolute demolition of the field at quail hollow! Oh yes and on the winning Ryder cup team! Please! Is this yet another case of protectionism by the pga tour or are they so desperate to win something! Wouldn't have something to do with Rory not joining the tour next year? Maybe the PGA tour just employs the same voting process as FIFA! Come on, fairs fair!

It was sharp and it was certainly accusative and controversial. But Westwood's grievance was merely the tip of an ever-growing iceberg of complaints against Rickie's elevation ahead of Rory.

Top golfer Graeme McDowell, that year's US Open champion, said he was also 'shocked' by the decision and argued that it should have gone Rory's way. He said, 'I agree with Lee that Rory was a lot more deserving than Rickie. You can't compare Rickie Fowler's season to Rory's – to win Quail Hollow in the style he did and to challenge in Major championships at the age of 21. Rory is one of the most talented players I've ever seen.' He added, 'But, at the end of the day it's just a title – it's nothing. Rory McIlroy will go on, I believe, to become one of the best players in the world, if not the best player, and win major championships.'

And what of the two men at the heart of the dispute? What exactly did Rickie think of his award – and was Rory actually upset or annoyed that he had lost out?

Rory acted swiftly to make it clear that, no, he was not

in the least peeved. Indeed, he was generous in his praise of Rickie. Rory said, 'It's fine. Look, I really didn't want it. I'm not a rookie. When I joined the PGA Tour, I was top 10 in the world. Rickie had an unbelievable year. He deserves it. I'm happy for Rickie that he got it.'

On the PGA's official website, it was argued that age should not be a barrier to winning the honour: 'The interpretation of a "true rookie" has not been a problem before. Vijay Singh won the award in 1993 when he was 30, having won in various parts of the world. Todd Hamilton was 39 when he won the award in 2004 on the strength of two victories, including the British Open. Hamilton had played almost exclusively in Asia until that year.'

And American golfer Dustin Johnson said he did not vote and added, 'Rickie's going to get votes because he had a decent year. But McIlroy is going to win. He's got to win.'

Dustin was then told that the issue had already been decided and that Rickie had triumphed, with Rory second. At that stage, a bemused Dustin added, 'Rickie won? Maybe [because] he's an American. I don't know why.'

At an official PGA media briefing at the start of December 2010, Rickie and Nationwide Tour Player of the Year Jamie Lovemark were asked how they felt after winning their awards. Rickie was reminded that he was the youngest recipient since Tiger Woods in 1996 – his twenty-one to Tiger's twenty that year. Rickie said, 'It's pretty cool. I guess I'm one year behind Tiger, but looking to try and make up some ground. It's been a lot of fun. Basically kind of started since Jamie and I were in the Play-offs last year, and we've both gone on to do pretty well. It's been pretty cool the first year out, and looking forward to the 2011 season, and for Jamie to finally join up with me out there.'

And when asked about how being a former student at Oklahoma State might have helped him reach such a stage in his burgeoning career, he replied, 'With the history that it has, we get to play one of the best college schedules throughout the year, and those opportunities to play against the other best college players in the nation definitely helped my game. It was definitely a stepping stone to help me be where I am today.'

If the Rookie of the Year award and the thrill of that late burst of brilliance at the Ryder Cup were the undoubted highlights of 2010 for Rickie, there were other moments of joy in the second half of his debut season as a pro. Rickie told friends that his appearance at the British Open in July 2010 was certainly in that category. In the fourth round, dressed all in orange from his cap to his shirt to his trousers, he made history at the seventeenth hole in the Open at St Andrews's Old Course. With a quite magical display, he putted home from 120 feet away on the green. It was part of his final round of sixty-seven and elevated him to a finish of tied fourteenth, despite a disappointing first round of seventy-nine. Rickie's final card for the event read 79–67–71–67, leaving him with a 4-under-par total of 284 and making him $87,840 richer. Not a bad weekend's work and one that certainly made the golfing fraternity in the UK sit up and realise that America had a new kid on the golfing block. One golf pundit, Lee Hayes, told me:

> He had the round of the day on the final day and it was great to see a youngster with such confidence, especially with that seventeenth hole shot, which was almost miraculous. This was a boy leaving a calling card, telling us he had arrived and that he was here to stay. Obviously there were early comparisons being made between Rickie and Rory Mac but that wasn't the main topic of conversation. Most people were just left open-mouthed at the kid's obvious confidence and talent – and the fact that he had the guts, skill and self-belief with that seventeenth-hole putt merely emphasised that he was going to be someone who would be around for a long time. He was colourful and he was talented and he left us with shots that would live long in the memory. It was refreshing to see a kid like that and his performance made us want more. We would definitely be keeping an eye out for him in future tournaments after his remarkable weekend's work at St Andrews – especially as he was in his debut year on the circuit. No doubt the best of Rickie Fowler was still to come and that was a tantalising prospect to leave the golfing world with as he headed home to America.

America's press pack was equally impressed by Rickie's feats at St Andrews and – inevitably, given the Land of the

Free's obsession with the new boy's image – his appearance. 'John Daly finally has some competition for worst outfit,' trumpeted the *Philadelphia Daily News*. They went on to say:

> Former Oklahoma State golfer Rickie Fowler did his best imitation of a giant pumpkin in the final round of the British Open on Sunday, decked out in hazard-cone orange from head to toe. Shoes, pants, belt, necklace, cap – even his Rolex had orange accents … He finished his first British Open in a tie for 14th at 4 under after posting his second 67 of the week Sunday. Fowler also made one of the best shots of the day, holing a putt of almost 130 feet from off the green for birdie on the 17th hole. Fowler tossed the ball into the crowd after he fished it out of the cup … Scrambling just to make the cut, Fowler rebounded with a 67 on Friday. He was below par each of his last three days, and had just two bogeys – none Sunday.

Rickie spoke of his delight at his final round at St Andrews while accepting that, with a touch more consistency, he could have ended much higher up the final leader board. He was bubbling with pride too when he talked of that wonderful putt on the seventeenth, saying, 'That was pretty cool. I think it's the longest putt I've ever made!'

There then followed a series of tournaments in which Rickie struggled to match his exploits of the British Open. He finished tied for thirty-third at the Bridgestone Invitational, tied for fifty-eighth at the US PGA, tied for thirty-sixth at the Barclays, tied for forty-first at the Deutsche Bank and tied for forty-fifth at the BMW Championship. Maybe the ever-looming prospect of that Ryder Cup event at the Celtic Manor had got to him; maybe it unnerved him a little as he prepared for the tournament. Certainly, his results at events post-Ryder Cup suggested he had regained his lost composure and was back on course. His final round at the Ryder Cup had lifted his spirits and made him a worldwide name. It has also been vital proof that he was worthy of playing with the world's best players and that, yes, he could now live with them on equal terms. It banished any latent self-questioning and gave Rickie the confidence to push forward as a pro of special talent and potential.

In mid-October, at his first event after the Ryder Cup, the bookmakers believed he would have a good chance of shrugging off his indifferent form in earlier PGA events – as did the pundits. The Associated Press (AP) even voiced the opinion that he might win his first PGA tournament, saying:

Rickie Fowler came close to winning his first PGA tournament at the Frys.com Open last year when it was held in Scottsdale, Arizona. He's hoping a different site will bring a different result. The event is making its Northern California debut on Thursday at the CordeValle Golf Club, about 30 miles south of San Jose, Calif. The colorful 21-year-old Fowler followed his impressive performance last season by finishing second twice this season, climbing to No. 33 in the rankings. It's his first tournament since going 1–1–2 at the Ryder Cup at Celtic Manor, where Team USA lost to Europe 14½–13½.

In 2010 he finished fourth at the Frys.com with a 13-under-par total of 271. He also pocketed $241,000 for his efforts. The previous season saw him end up tied for second. His 2010 highlight came when he made three birdies on the back nine – and his sponsors, Puma, were quick to congratulate him: 'Puma Golfer, Rickie Fowler, birdied three of his final five holes at The Frys.com Open to finish in 4th place. The birdies put him 13 under for the tournament. Great job Rickie!'

Rickie admitted afterwards that finishing in the top five at the Frys for the second year running had boosted his confidence still further after his fine finish at the Ryder Cup. He said:

Every time I get in contention I keep feeling a little more comfortable than the last time. If we keep putting ourselves in the same spot, hopefully it will pay off in the long run. I hung in there through the front nine [on his final round]. I played pretty good, especially with the rain coming up. I wanted to put myself in a good position for the back nine, and felt like I had a good chance and right where I wanted to be the last few holes. I hit a lot of really good putts and had a lot of really good opportunities. A lot of good putts but they just didn't go in.

Maybe not but his form was clearly picking up again after that pre-Ryder Cup low. A fourth-place finish at any event was not to be scoffed at and he followed it shortly afterwards with a tied for fifth place at the Asia Pacific Classic in Malaysia and a tied for third place at the Children's Miracle Network Classic. The former event took place at the Tanjong Course in Singapore. Rickie carded a 4-round 14-under-par total of 270 and enhanced his bank balance by a further $237,500. In the latter he did even better, finishing tied for third in the final PGA tournament of the year. Rickie enjoyed his four rounds at the Magnolia course in Lake Buena Vista, Florida, and enjoyed even more that he had finished the campaign on such a high.

Afterwards he let the press into a little secret: that he had been casting glances at the leader board as he headed toward the conclusion of his weekend's work and that he often did so. Many golfers avoid checking the board because it can distract them or deflate them – but not so the all-American poster boy of golf. He admitted, 'I always look at boards. I like to know my position and I don't think it really affects my play so much. I like to know when I'm behind. Gets me fired up a bit and makes me want to make birdies. I was looking to make a few more birdies on the back nine, but it was still a solid day of golf.'

And he was asked to give his reflections upon what had

been, overall, a wonderful first season as a pro on the PGA Tour. He said, 'It's been awesome. To get my PGA Tour card right after turning pro was big, and it was great to secure my card for next year early on in the season. It took some of the pressure off me – freed me up for the rest of the season. It gave me some more opportunities to go through the FedExCup and then to get picked for the Ryder Cup team. So the only thing that was really missing is a win – otherwise it has been a great year.'

It almost turned out to be even better – a million times better to be precise! Rickie took part in a three-way play-off after the tournament in a bid to win the $1 million Kodak Challenge. This is a season-long contest with PGA Tour players taking their best score on eighteen of thirty designated holes for the year. Rickie had approached the Children's Miracle tournament at Disney World full of confidence after being in pole position for most of the season. Indeed, in mid-September the PGA had put out a press release explaining just what the event was, how it was conducted, and eulogising how Rickie was setting the pace in his rookie pro campaign – yet at the same time pointing out just how difficult it would be for him to maintain his lead. The release read like this:

PGA Tour Rookie of the Year contender Rickie Fowler currently leads the Kodak Challenge at 14 under. Fowler has held the top position on the Kodak Challenge leader board since the final round of the Verizon Heritage tournament at Harbour Town Links in Hilton Head, S.C. on April 18. The Ryder Cup team member leads a strong field of contenders into the final stages of the Kodak Challenge.

Now in its second year, the Kodak Challenge celebrates beautiful holes and memorable moments on the PGA Tour, challenging players to perform their best on 30 designated Kodak Challenge holes. The player with the lowest cumulative score on his best 18 Kodak Challenge holes will win $1 million. Kevin Streelman claimed the first Kodak Challenge title at the PGA Tour's final event of the 2009 season, the Children's Miracle Network Classic in Lake Buena Vista. Twenty-nine PGA Tour players are currently within four strokes of Rickie Fowler's field-leading pace. Troy Merritt sits just two shots behind Fowler at 12 under, while Tim Petrovic, Brandt Snedeker, Carl Pettersson, Jimmy Walker, Lee Janzen and John Senden are only three strokes off the lead at 11 under. With two par-5s and three par-4s in the final five holes, players within striking distance of Fowler have plenty of chances to make a run at the $1 million Kodak Challenge prize.

The PGA's assessment would ultimately prove prophetic. At the end of the day, it was Merritt who pocketed the $1 million cheque after a seventeenth-hole play-off with Rickie and Aaron Baddeley.

But to finish in the top three of a season-long event was

not to be sniffed at. OK, Rickie had lost out on the $1 million but, at the same time, he had cemented his position still further in the elite world of PGA golfers. The year 2010 had been both a massive success and a signpost of things to come. As Christmas 2010 loomed, Rickie headed off to his girlfriend Alexandra Browne's house in Florida for the festive season. The eighteen-year-old was the daughter of Rickie's fellow pro, Olin, and Rickie enjoyed being with her as she 'kept him grounded' and they had great fun days out together. Indeed, Alexandra organised Rickie a fantastic pre-Christmas fishing expedition in the Keys, much to his delight. And as Christmas and then the New Year of 2011 dawned, Rickie could reflect on a year of laying down markers and anticipate the likelihood of progressing further and sealing more glory in his second year on the pro circuit.

The boy had arrived as a star – no doubt about it.

CHAPTER SIX

SECOND-SEASON
SYNDROME

Having announced his arrival on the professional scene in his first year on the PGA Tour, Rickie began 2011 fully confident that he would build upon his successes over the past twelve months. He had shown that he was good enough to mix with the big boys and now his plan was to develop and win his first tournament. Well, that may have been the plan but its implementation was an altogether different subject, for in 2011 Rickie's results would suggest that he'd had a mixed bag of a year, with a few real statements of intent mingling with many disappointments.

In the music business, pundits often refer to 'Difficult Second Album Syndrome' when describing a singer or band's traditional struggle to better – or even match – the often-ground-breaking efforts of their first album. Rickie would suffer the same struggle after a first season that brimmed with promise and brilliance. His task now was to avoid the golfing version of that – Second-Season Syndrome.

So maybe it was no real surprise that his year got off to an indifferent start and that he struggled to build, let alone maintain, momentum; more often than not, he seemed on the brink of greatness, only to fall away and end up with the also-rans. His first event of the new campaign highlights this topsy-turvy nature of his second season as a professional golfer. After a wonderful Christmas holiday spent with his girlfriend and her parents, Rickie headed off to the Farmers Insurance Open in San Diego, California, full of confidence and full of beans. He believed that this would be the season when he would, indeed, land that first title – so why not go for it in the very first tournament of the year?

Before the tournament, Rickie was asked how he hoped the new season would pan out. He admitted that he was confident and that he hoped simply to improve on his first campaign. He said, 'My expectations this year are to continue playing well. I had a great rookie year and a lot of fun getting my feet wet on the PGA Tour! I would also like to get my first win out of the way.'

A sure sign of how he was maturing as a person came when he made it clear he did not see himself as a big celebrity; that he was still the kid from next door. No way did he want a gulf to exist between him and his fans. The main things in his life were constant: his family, his friends, his golf and his fans. Speaking at a press conference, Rickie put it this way: 'I do get noticed in public a little more now, which is cool. I like people coming up and asking for autographs and pictures. But I don't look at myself any differently – and I'm not trying to act any differently. I want to be a good role model for my fans and young kids in the game of golf – and I am trying to get more people interested in the game of golf.'

Of course, he was also maturing as a golfer – that much became clear when he said he had learned the importance of one characteristic that could prove vital to his hopes: patience. Rickie said:

One of the main things I have learned in this past year is patience. That was key to me playing well in the few events that I did so. There were a few events I felt I struggled in and patience was probably a part of the reason I did struggle. In a normal round or normal tournament you are playing on Thursday and Friday and Saturday to set yourself up for the Sunday.

The tournament is not won on Thursday or Friday and you have to be patient and bide your time. A few times over the year I snuck into a good finish – top five or top 10 – because I was able to hang around the first three days and put in a solid round on the Sunday.

So did he have the patience to pull off that first win at the Farmers at the end of January 2011? Well, he certainly had the determination and positivity to try and he did get off to a fine start at the event in San Diego. Rickie carded a seven-under-par first round score of sixty-five. That left him tied for second place with Alex Prugh, both of them one shot behind early pacesetter Kang Sung-hoon. The situation was one Rickie felt sure he could profit from, tucked in nicely behind the leader and ready to pounce as play continued. The previous year, of course, he had opened with a sound sixty-seven on the North Course before three rounds of seventy on the South Course. That left him in a tied for fifth finish. So with that opening sixty-five – which was his first round of the new season – he was more than confident that he could progress to an even better finish this time around.

He was certainly pleased with his opening round, which included a birdie on the second hole and some fine putting as he made the turn at five-under-par. He admitted that he had felt nervous going into his first tournament of the year – and that, yes, he was maybe a little rusty after five weeks off, time he had spent in Florida with his girlfriend and other pals. Well, if a sixty-five first round is what Rickie does when he is a bit nervy, it would remain to be seen what he could achieve when he was fully focused!

Rickie was disappointed to finish tied for twentieth after that brilliant opening salvo, with rounds of 71, 73 and 74. Sure, he had begun the year richer with a $65,000 cheque for finishing twentieth but he had hoped to finish much higher up the leader board. At least he had the consolation of seeing his pal Bubba Watson clinch the top prize, with Phil Mickelson a stroke behind the winner. *Southland Golf Magazine* best summed up Rickie's disappointment, saying, 'A tie for 20th certainly isn't anything to sneer at on the

PGA Tour but Murrieta's Fowler backed into that slot after positioning himself in contention through 36 holes. He had made winning a priority during his sophomore season on Tour, but weekend rounds of 73–74 aren't going to net him any trophies.'

That analysis was tough but fair – Rickie had, indeed, made it quite clear he was going for glory in this second pro season and so finishing so low down the leader board was certainly not part of the master plan. There was one spin-off from his excursions in the event – Farmers Insurance announced they would be sponsoring the charity video starring Rickie, Ben Crane, Bubba Watson (the winner of the 2011 Farmers Insurance Open) and Hunter Mahan. The foursome were already creating headlines with their band, Golf Boys, and were now releasing their world-premiere music video, 'Oh Oh Oh'. The involvement of Farmers Insurance was a real shot in the arm for Rickie and his fellow fundraisers as they now agreed to donate $1,000 for every 100,000 views of the video on YouTube. That delighted Rickie who, as we have already noted, was extremely generous with both his time and his money when it came to helping charitable causes.

A week after the Farmers Insurance tournament, Rickie would finish slightly further up the scale at the Waste Management Open in Phoenix, Arizona. His four-round card saw him post 70, 62, 69 and 70 and boost his bank balance by $111,000 as he ended up tied for thirteenth. But he was obviously highly delighted with that second round of sixty-two – it emphasised his quality and just how good he could be when he was in the mood. Rickie equalled the course record on the back nine with his score of twenty-nine, and a bogey-free round meant he was right in the mix as the tournament approached its weekend finale. 'I'm right where I want to be,' Fowler said after his bogey-free round. 'I started off with a missed putt on ten, but right from there we made a good putt on eleven and got it going. It was fun. Obviously I want to have a chance going into the last two rounds, and most importantly the last round, so we'll try to go out tomorrow and play well and get ourselves in contention.'

Unfortunately, he could not keep up the good work. He fell back down the field and left Arizona frustrated. In this season of missed opportunities, this would be a regular emotion: the idea of 'what could have been' and many a dream of glory dashed. It was a similar story at the Northern Trust Open a fortnight later as Rickie finished tied for thirty-fifth and only had the joy of a third round of 68 to savour as he exited LA's Riviera Country Club with a one-under-par final card of 283.

Then came something approaching Rickie Fowler at his hypnotic, wonderful-to-watch best as he teed off in the Accenture World Matchplay event as he beat Phil Mickelson 6&5 in the second round. *The Guardian* summed up how it was almost like a changing of the old guard for the new as Rickie stormed to victory, going on to say:

Phil Mickelson could only laugh as he departed the World Match Play, a middle-aged man with a paunch hammered in the second round by Rickie Fowler, a feisty lad in a shocking pink shirt and outsized cap. "He is going to do great things for American golf," the big left-hander said of the twenty-two-year-old who had just beaten him 6&5. Few would bet against that now.

It is a fool's errand to read too much into one round of golf, especially matchplay golf, but, as the first world golf championship of the season heads towards its climax in Arizona, the symbolism of the moment was impossible to ignore. The young Turks are no longer coming, they have arrived, ready to overthrow the two players, Mickelson and Tiger Woods, who have ruled the sport for so long.

Indeed, they were – Rickie and Rory Mac were the pacesetters in the new order. They were the two personalities who could conceivably carry golf into a new golden age after the Tiger Woods period.

Rickie came up against Matt Kuchar in the third round but, after the dizzying exploits of his commendable win over Mickelson, he now hit the buffers, losing out on a quarter-final spot after Kuchar triumphed 2&1. But, as always, Rickie was magnanimous in defeat, simply accepting that Kuchar had been the better player on the day: 'I had a couple of stretches where I wasn't playing too good. I'm disappointed about eleven and twelve, missing some little up-and-downs and short putts that I thought definitely helped the match go the other way. I tried to fight at the end but Kuch just made some putts today. And he made them when he needed to and obviously closed me out on seventeen, with a five-footer.'

It was clearly starting off to be a difficult second season. In the same way that rock bands were often derailed by DSAS – as mentioned above, the so-called Difficult Second Album Syndrome after a rip-roaring debut record – so Rickie was now finding it hard to maintain some consistency in his game. Sure, there were occasional flashes of brilliance, but they all too often tapered off into disappointing finales. And the start of March 2011 saw this narrative repeated once again as an initially buoyant Rickie ended up missing the cut with a second-round two-over-par seventy-two. It remained a case of one-step forwards, one or two steps backwards as he tried to find the right balance between certainty, over-confidence and recklessness in his approach.

One week on and Rickie's mood swung from disappointment to optimism yet again as he produced some fine shots at the Cadillac Championship in Doral, Florida. This time Rickie would begin his assault on the title with two poor rounds – carding a seventy-one and a seventy-three – before doing the business on his final two rounds. He hit a 68 in the third round and a brilliant 66, which was the joint best score in the whole of the final round, to finish on a 10-under-par total of 278. That final-round achievement meant he finished tied for eighth and that he took away a nice fat cheque for $200,000.

But Rickie was more pleased at hitting that final-round sixty-six, as only he and Tiger Woods had achieved such a low round on the final day. Woods, of course, had won the event many times and it was an immense boost to Rickie's confidence that he had managed to match his legendary fellow American. He told friends afterwards that he had 'really enjoyed' the challenge and that he 'was aware' of the situation with Tiger. Like many of the young Turks now starting to dominate the world of pro golf, he retained a respect for Woods despite the older man's personal-life indiscretions. The Tiger was still the yardstick by which Rickie and Rory McIlroy judged their own development on the greens – he was, after all, one of the finest golfers ever, with a record of wins and achievements that remained impossible to ignore. Tiger may have erred in his private life but he was still the man to beat; the king to dethrone for the youngsters coming through the ranks. So to equal his final round in Doral meant a great deal to Rickie. It showed once again that the boy was coming of age – that he was now ready to rival the greats of the game and eventually supplant them.

'It's true that Woods was still the main man,' a golfing insider told me, going on to say:

Sure, he had made mistakes in his life – and that, in turn, had obviously affected his golf. But there was still the feeling on the tour that Tiger would eventually find his level again. That when he sorted out his problems and found some sort of peace again, his game would improve back to the level of greatness he once took for granted. So tyros like Fowler and McIlroy were never complacent in his company on the greens: they knew that, if he managed to hit form, he would take some stopping. Meanwhile, the youngsters used the time that he was struggling to move their own games forward so that, when the day of Tiger's renaissance arrived, they would also have moved up a step or two. They were never scared of Woods but they all had a respect for his talent.

Yet after Rickie's sterling efforts to match The Tiger in that final round of the Cadillac, he struggled to match those levels in the next three-and-a-half months. If mid-March had seen him stake a claim for potential greatness at Doral, the period that followed up to the start of June 2011 saw him battle vainly for some consistency of quality in his game. In nine tournaments following the Doral, he never once appeared in the top ten on the final leader board. A pundit pal of mine pointed out to me that there was something of a pattern to Rickie's golf in these first couple of years as a professional; that he would give a top-notch display of golf and finish well up the field, only to follow it with a series of disappointing results.

I put it down to growing pains – that you could not realistically expect a young man of twenty-one who had not long ago joined the pro ranks to consistently hit the top ten; that he would need a period of coming to terms with the step-up and that he would improve with experience. To an extent, it had been the same with Rory McIlroy and now Rickie Fowler was also having to dig deep to keep himself positive and to banish those lingering moments of doubt. Luckily, as we have noted throughout, Rickie was a man who was predominantly of a positive nature. He believed in himself and in his ability and, whenever he did go through a bleak patch, he would tell friends it was just a phase – that he would eventually turn things around with hard work, practice and determination. One standout example of his struggles during that period of 2011 was his showing at the Masters in Augusta towards the end of April. Rickie tied for thirty-eighth after finishing with a 1-over-par total of 289. Of course, he was disappointed with his finish but, being the sort of guy who always prefers to see the glass half-full, he said he had enjoyed playing the course and that he had experienced some highs too. He had headed to Augusta early and prepared in the same way he prepares for any tournament – by participating in a practice round with a couple of friends. On this occasion, he had worked his way around the course with Bubba Watson and Peter Uihlein.

That had helped him settle and, as tee-off approached, Rickie sounded confident and relaxed as he spoke to the press corps. This would be his debut at arguably the most celebrated tournament in America – certainly one of the most legendary. 'This is most definitely a dream come true,' Rickie conceded, continuing to say:

To have a chance to play in my first Masters is something I've dreamed about since I was a little kid. I watched plenty of Masters growing up. The green jacket is obviously something that means quite a bit in the golfing community. To have a chance to be in the tournament and with playing well right now, I feel like if I go into the week with high expectations – there's a chance I could be walking up to 18 in contention. That is something I've dreamed about – the special walk up to 18. Just to be a part of this week is pretty cool.

Rickie was not naïve – he knew it would take some performance to end up in the top ten, let alone win it! He added, 'It's not an easy golf course to just go out and learn. It takes some time. And it's a Major. So, you're going to see the seasoned veterans who usually do well – like Tom Watson and Fred Couples. Hopefully we can get a couple young guys on top this year.'

Well, there would be one young player who took the course for storm on the first three rounds – but it wasn't Rickie. It was his rival Rory McIlroy, who made all the headlines around the world. The Northern Ireland ace looked on course for a certain Masters win as he led by four shots going into the final round but could not maintain that lead. McIlroy blew it on the back nine as he carded a poor eight-over-par eighty and turned what looked like certain victory into a demoralising defeat. To be fair, the Irishman was of the same mettle as Rickie – he remained positive and shrugged his shoulders when asked how low he felt at losing out on the coveted green jacket. 'I was still one shot ahead going into the tenth and then things went all pear-shaped after that,' Rory said. 'But I'll get over it. I'll have plenty more chances – I know that.'

Asked to explain just why he 'choked', Rory added:

I don't think I can put it down to anything else than part of the learning curve. Hopefully, if I can get myself back into this position pretty soon, I will handle it a little bit better. It will be pretty tough for me for the next few days but I will get over it – I'll be fine. There are a lot worse things that can happen in your life. Shooting a bad score in the last round of a golf tournament is nothing in comparison to what other people go through.

Getting applauded up onto the greens, I was almost a little embarrassed at some points. But the support I had here was fantastic and I really appreciate it. I lost a lot of confidence with my putting, but I just hit a poor tee shot on ten and sort of unravelled from there. I'll have plenty more chances I know and, hopefully, it will build a bit of character in me as well.

Rory's attitude was excellent – both he and Rickie were of the same determined, no-regrets mindset. They did their best at a tournament and, whether that was good enough to do well or not, moved on to the next tournament and the next challenge.

South African Charl Schwartzel was the man who profited from Rory's meltdown, winning his first Major crown.

Rickie witnessed first-hand the explosive start of McIlroy

as he was paired with him for the opening round. At a press conference afterwards, Rickie had this to say about the pairing and his own start: 'I got off to a very rough start – didn't make any birdies until 14. Then I made four in the last five holes so it was definitely a nice way to finish. It was nice playing alongside Rory, who looked like he was doing everything right. I saw him get a few balls in the hole and that definitely helped me make some putts in the end.' Those quotes help sum up the decent kind of guy Rickie Fowler has always been – his words of praise about his number-one rival once again highlighted his generous nature. This was a young man who was determined to reach the top but who would not resort to mind games or catcalls when the subject of his rivals was brought up in press conferences. He wanted to do things right and was certainly one of the most open, friendly and kindly players on what has always been a competitive circuit.

He also made it clear that he viewed Rory as a friend, rather than an enemy, as some pundits were now trying to portray their relationship. Rickie told a press conference how he and the Irishman got on well and, indeed, had spent some time 'hanging out' together: 'I like to talk on the golf course, I like to hang out, have a good time. Rory spent some time down in Jupiter in Florida recently – which is where I live – and we talked about stuff to do down there. Fishing, fun stuff, not really talking too much golf.'

Rickie carded a seventy on his first round at Augusta and followed it with a promising sixty-nine on the second, taking him five-under-par. Unfortunately, he would then suffer a lapse that saw him finish with rounds of seventy-six and seventy-four. That promising beginning had once again been lost in the latter stages of an event: he remained a work in progress: a player who was well on the way to stardom but one who also still needed to find that elusive consistency in his natural game.

He had sounded so enthusiastic and confident after his second round too, saying how much he was enjoying his maiden outing at the Masters: 'I had a lot of fun out there with my group. Both Rory and Jason [Day] have been putting up some good rounds in the last two days. Jason snuck up on us today with 8-under, and it was fun to watch. But being around good golf definitely helps. Obviously I was just trying to keep up with those guys and it helps being around the guys playing well. I was sneaking up there at 5-under and really looking forward to getting into this weekend.'

Given such an optimistic attitude, it was, therefore, a bit of a letdown that Rickie could not maintain the pressure on the leading pack over the final two rounds. He had also said that he believed he 'had a chance' of winning, so to finish thirty-eighth was a disappointment for the boy and his growing army of fans. Of course, it was the same story – if not even worse, given his commanding early lead – for McIlroy, whom Rickie termed 'a veteran, even though he is younger than me and Jason!'

Despite the blowouts in the second stage of the event, there was little doubt that Rickie, Rory and Jason had truly arrived on the big stage – they had made a real name for themselves. Indeed, the Masters' official website confirmed that scenario after the first thirty-six holes, pointing out that:

The trio's combined age is 66 years, and they drew a following of younger patrons who inspired a move up the leader board as quickly as the players like to walk around a course. They combined to make 34 birdies in the first 36 holes to position themselves in first place at 10-under (McIlroy), second at 8-under (Day) and tied for seventh at 5-under (Fowler).

With his first-round 65, McIlroy was the youngest 18-hole leader in Tournament history. Seve Ballesteros was age 23 years and 1 day when he held the first-round lead on the way to the 1980 Masters title. Ballesteros shot 66 in the first round that year. Tiger Woods, only three back after a Friday 66, set the record in 1997 as the youngest 36-hole leader at age 21 years, 3 months and 14 days.

There was no doubt about it: the young ones were on the march, led by Rickie, Rory and Jason. It would take a little time before they dominated the sport but one day the three of them would do just that. Rickie packed his bags at the end of the Masters but did not leave with his head down, precisely because he knew that his day would come: he knew he simply had to be patient and keep on doing what he was doing and that he would arrive when the time was right. He needed to be more consistent and work at his game – and that was exactly what he would do during the second half of 2011.

There followed a series of disappointing results after the Masters and prior to the British Open in July, best exemplified by him missing the cut in The Players Championship and the US Open (in the latter of which McIlroy would truly announce his arrival as a force to be reckoned with by winning) but by the end of June, Rickie's game stirred. He finished tied for thirteenth in the AT&T National at Newton Square, Pennsylvania, and declared himself fit and ready to make his mark in the British Open in the middle of July. Rickie Fowler was on his way to Royal St George's in Sandwich, Kent and was determined to serve up a meal fit for a king... and he would do just that.

CHAPTER SEVEN

PUTTING DOWN A MARKER

For once, Rickie felt slightly nervous as he headed 'across the pond' to England for the British Open in July 2011. He had bombed in the Masters and had missed the cut in the other two Majors that had already taken place that year – The Players Championship and the US Open. Plus there was the little matter of his biggest rival winning the latter event. Yes, Rory McIlroy had banished his Masters blues by securing his first Major in that tournament. So the pressure was somewhat on Rickie as he touched down at Heathrow in London. His own year had been one of ups and downs – showing potential in some events but also struggling to maintain the high standard he had set himself in others – so there was much riding on his showing at Royal St George's in Sandwich.

He arrived early in the Kent countryside to acquaint himself with the course, enjoying a day of practice and geeing himself up for action. He was keen, committed and out to show that he was a match for Rory and the other big beasts on the golfing circuit. It would take some display to elevate himself into that exalted group; he would certainly need to step up a level or two if he were to make an impression.

And Rickie would do just that. He came, he saw and he conquered at Sandwich, recording his best finish in a Major (tied for 5th) and finally delivering on his immense potential and talent in front of the world's cameras. He carded a total of 280, consisting of rounds of 70, 70, 68 and 72. He even managed to outshine McIlroy, who had been the pre-tournament favourite after his US Open victory. Rickie had teed off with Rory and Ernie Els in the first round on a windy and wet Thursday at Royal St George's. The young golfer had admitted at a general press conference before the tournament began that he was thrilled to be alongside Rory after his US Open win; he said it provided him with a superb opportunity to measure his own development. 'Rory is a step or two ahead of me right now in professional golf,' he explained. 'He turned pro a little bit younger than I did and he's off and running and doing well. It was fun to watch him at Congressional. It showed what was possible. It was an impressive week and inspiring for any golfer, especially for us young guys.'

After his first round of seventy, Rickie admitted that he was pleased with his day's work and that he was 'having a blast' working his way around the course with his old pal Rory. Rickie said, 'The course is playing great. You hit good shots, you're going to get rewarded. It's fun out there. I'm having a good time. It was a fun pairing. Rory and I always enjoy playing together and it's always fun to play with Ernie [Els]. But when you're playing well, hitting good shots and getting off to a good start, it's not too hard to have a good time.'

The *Daily Telegraph* made the telling comment that Rickie and Rory seemed to be moving towards the top together and that, on this occasion, Rickie had overshadowed his Northern Irish pal:

Ever since they first faced off in the 2007 Walker Cup at Royal County Down, McIlroy and Fowler have forged a compelling dynamic: the great European hope head to head with the photogenic poster-boy of American golf. It was Fowler's turn to eclipse his rival on Thursday, courtesy of an eventful 70. He shaped irons and angled chip-and-runs with an imagination that belied his background on more manicured US layouts.

But the main thing was that he himself had played a good first round – one that left him in contention with the big guns of golf. Rickie declared himself 'well happy' with his round and said it filled him with confidence for the weekend. It was important not to put in a poor opening statement, as it was very hard to make a stake for a title on the remaining days. A poor first round would leave you lacking confidence and put you in a position where you would always be playing 'catch-up'. 'To get off to a good start makes me feel good and to go out there and play the way I did makes me feel confident going into tomorrow,' Rickie said. 'It's always nice to get off to a good start in a Major. You can't win it the first day, but you can obviously put yourself pretty far behind – like I did last year.'

Rickie's real moment of glory would come in the third round on the Saturday as he went round in sixty-eight, while Rory was struggling to match him with a seventy-four. The pair would laugh and tease each other as they vied for supremacy around St George's, but on this occasion it would be Rickie who would have the last laugh. After that super round of sixty-eight, he said, 'I had quite a bit of fun out there today. I love playing links golf and this is only the second time I've played in the Open Championship – but I got a real taste of links golf for the first time at the 2007 Walker Cup at County Down.' He continued, 'It's just the way I grew up, learning how to hit different shots, and that's how you've got to play around here, depending on the weather conditions or how the wind is blowing.'

Even the Open's own website heaped praise on Rickie, saying he had put himself in contention for the Claret Jug with 'the round of the day.' They went on to say: 'His remarkable two under par 68 brought him swiftly through the field from joint 19th into a tie for third place with Thomas Bjorn.'

And McIlroy admitted that he had found it difficult to stay with Rickie and that he was not surprised to find himself six shots behind him after the round. 'This tournament, more so than anything else, you need to get a good draw and it just hasn't worked out for me this week,' Rory said. 'It was really tough out there this morning, and I felt, for the first thirteen holes, to get through those in two over par was a pretty decent effort. Then to give two shots away on fourteen was very disappointing. I tried to make a couple of birdies coming down the last four holes, but wasn't able to do it, and I think seventy-four was the best I could manage.'

The Northern Irishman may have been disappointed with his own game but he did not allow that to cloud his praise for Rickie. He said, 'Rickie played really well. He's such a natural player and he's got a lot of feel, so he controls his ball flight very well. And he's got a great short game. He gets it up and down when he needs to, holes good putts at the right times. A 68 out there in those conditions was very impressive.' Those were generous words from a man who, like Rickie, held no grudges against fellow pros: the new generation of golfing superstars were united in their civilised approach to the game and each other. They may have looked flashy and super-confident but that was underpinned with respect for fellow players, good manners on the course and eloquent tributes to victors when they were hurting inside after a disappointing round or tournament.

Rickie said it had been 'great fun' working alongside Rory, although the conditions – with wind and rain making accuracy tricky – were among 'the worst' he had played in. He admitted that he and Rory had shared a bit of banter as they went round the course and that it had been a great motivation for him to see how Rory worked and to try his best to rival him. 'I talked to him briefly about his US Open win,' Rickie said. 'I just asked him if he had a good time, and he said he had fun. It was a lot of fun to watch him. It definitely motivated me and gave me more confidence because we are a similar age and at a similar part of our career. I'd say he's a step ahead of me. He's got a couple wins and a Major under his belt.'

At the post-round press conference Rickie also laughed off suggestions that his rivalry with Rory could turn them against each other. He made it clear that McIlroy was a friend as well as someone he viewed as a brilliant golfer, saying:

People always ask about our friendship or if we enjoy playing together. We love playing together. It's always fun playing with someone that you enjoy … being around. But at the same time we're trying to beat each other. It's a friendly rivalry. I dealt with it through high school and college with teammates. You're teammates but you go out there in a tournament and you're trying to beat each other.

Obviously I'm trying to beat him on a daily basis and he usually plays pretty well and puts himself in contention. So I felt like, if we went out today and beat Rory, we'd be in a good spot. Unfortunately, he made a double late and struggled a little bit. But I felt I played well and got my job done today.

He also said he would love to win the Open – it would be his first Major triumph and, indeed, his first win as a professional if he could pull it off. 'I'd love for my first win to be a Major and I'd love for it to be here,' he said. 'I'm playing every tournament to win, to be in contention and to give it a shot, so I'm in a perfect place going into tomorrow. I felt that I played really well today and it's going to give me a lot of confidence going into tomorrow. I just need to make some putts to stay in contention.'

He remained in contention on the final day but, ultimately, didn't top the lot. McIlroy's fellow Northern Irishman, Darren Clarke, ended up the victor, finishing at five-under for the tournament after an even-par final round. Few would begrudge the popular veteran his moment of glory – certainly not Rickie, who offered him his genuine congratulations. It meant a lot to Clarke – it was his first Major win as he finished three strokes clear of Phil Mickelson and Dustin Johnson, who tied for second. Clarke was no longer even in the world's top 100 but he said he would certainly enjoy his night of glory and 'end up hungover.' After lifting the Claret Jug he said, 'It's been a dream since I've been a kid to win the Open, like any kid's dream is, and I'm able to do it, which just feels incredible. We're blessed to have two fantastic players in Rory and GMac and I've just come along, the only guy coming along behind them.'

Thomas Bjorn of Sweden finished fourth and then came Rickie Fowler, tied for fifth with fellow Americans Anthony Kim and Chad Campbell. And not only had Rickie put in a more than creditable performance, he had also ended the tournament well ahead of McIlroy. Rory could only manage a tied for twenty-fifth finish, and left Sandwich complaining about the weather and how he preferred playing in the warmth: 'I'm not a fan of golf tournaments that are, you know, the outcome's predicted so much by the weather. It's not my sort of golf. Just wait for a year when the weather's nice. My game is suited for basically every golf course and most conditions, but these conditions I just don't enjoy playing in really. That's the bottom line. I'd rather play when it's eighty degrees and sunny and not much wind. There's no point in changing your game for one week a year.'

Rory is a great guy and a fantastic golfer but his words clearly reflected his disappointment at not being able to deliver when it counted.

Certainly there were no such downbeat emotions when Rickie was asked how he felt after the weekend's events at Sandwich. He said he was just pleased to have been in the mix as the final round unravelled, that it had been the first time he had negotiated such a high finish in a Major and that he very much 'liked the feeling.' 'I haven't really been in contention come Sunday in a Major, so it definitely felt nice. I felt really good today. It's been two solid tournaments in a row for me. I put myself in the last group at AT&T and then had another good week here. A lot of positives today but I just missed out with a couple putts. If they had gone in I could have got some momentum going. I just struggled with that.'

Jeff Cohn of the *Bleacher Report* made the point that the final outcome at Royal St George's showed the strength of American golf and that Rickie Fowler could now be seen as a genuine contender to win a Major. Cohn continued:

The runners-up were Phil Mickelson and Dustin Johnson, who each ended two under [par]. This proves that Clarke wasn't the only winner today – Dustin Johnson got the second place prize that he thought he had nearly secured in the 2010 PGA Championship; Phil Mickelson proved that he could overcome challenges and succeed in a tournament that never treated him nicely before, and that hard work and patience pays off; and they both proved that Americans are now serious contenders in golf and may win many Majors in the near future. Rickie Fowler and Anthony Kim are also examples of this – they tied for fifth place.'

Three weeks later Rickie showed that his top-five finish at the British Open was no fluke; that, yes, he was really running into some top-class form right now, as he finished in a tie for second at the WGC-Bridgestone Invitational in Akron, Ohio behind winner Adam Scott. That impressive showing also hauled him high up the world rankings, to number twenty-eight. Rickie was delighted with his showing and that he had put in one of the best final-round displays – and scores – of his short but burgeoning professional career. At a general press conference he admitted:

I've been playing a lot better the last month or two and this is really the first time for a while that I've played a good final round. It was nice to go out and shoot a bogey-free four-under-par. I was in contention at the AT&T and at the Open Championship. After those two Sunday final rounds, I just knew I had to be a lot more patient and make sure that I was fully committed to every shot and think everything through and make sure I was ready to hit each shot. We did it today, did it well, and it resulted in a bogey-free 66.

Adam Scott had won with an impressive 17-under-par total of 263, 4 strokes ahead of Rickie and Luke Donald. The result meant Rickie would bank a cheque for another $461,770 and it was clear that he was moving closer and closer towards that elusive first victory as a professional. His composure, his attitude and his fierce determination to chalk up that victory – with extra sessions practising and perfecting his strokes – would then help him to make headlines in the one remaining Major of the year: the PGA Championship. He didn't emerge victorious but his play on the third day had the pundits and fellow players gasping and applauding. Rickie carded 74–69–75–68 to finish with a 6-over par total of 286 and a disappointing tied for fifty-first finish.

But his work on that third day convinced many people that Rickie could chalk up that breakthrough win if he could reproduce the form he showed then. Rickie scored three birdies in the first five holes – a quite brilliant achievement. Unfortunately, he would also later record two triple-bogeys.

A couple of months on from his successful showings in the British Open and the Bridgestone, he would finally achieve that maiden win – much to his delight, as well as that of his family and his close friends. It would be one of the great moments in his career and victory would be all the sweeter because the man he overwhelmed was none other than his closest rival of 2011 and the man who would be his closest rival in the future – Rory McIlroy.

CHAPTER EIGHT

THE FIRST BIG WIN

October 2011 would be a month that Rickie Fowler would never forget. For that was the month when he finally nailed his first win on the pro circuit. Sure, he had chalked up many triumphs as an amateur but this one meant so much more, for it proved once and for all that he was worthy of being mentioned as the future of golf with the likes of McIlroy and that he no longer needed to be treated with kid gloves by his fellow players. He had shown he had talent, guts and the commitment needed to be a top golfer and that this was truly the start of something big.

Rickie had hinted that he was coming ever closer to a victory with that brilliant tied for fifth finish at the British Open in Sandwich back in July and the subsequent tied for second finish at Bridgestone the following month. Typical of Rickie's topsy-turvy season, he then flopped at the Barclays, the Deutsche Bank and the BMW Championship at the end of August and into September. He could only manage a tied for fifty-second finish at the Barclays and the Deutsche, and forty-eighth in the BMW.

The Deutsche encapsulated how Rickie had blown hot and cold during the 2011 season. He started well, only to fall away at the back end of the tournament.

His play was improving but his consistency left something to be desired. He knew he was heading in the right direction and that he was becoming a better golfer but it was difficult to predict if he would bomb and miss the cut, or battle through to a top-five finish. Obviously he was aware of the nature of his season but, always being an optimist, he preferred to talk about his successes rather than his setbacks. That was typical of the man: he believed that the future would be brighter if you focused on your strengths.

So it was at the Deutsche that he told how he was generally pleased with his progress and with his big results in recent months. He said, 'I've been playing well the last two-and-a-half, three months or so. I've put myself in position a few times and in contention, finished tied for second at the WGC, finished fifth at the Open Championship, so it's been nice to be back in contention and to feel the nerves, get the juices flowing.'

I – and many other pundits – found Rickie's attitude refreshing and admired him for seeing the positives. He was a good man to be paired with on the course and just as vibrant and clearly happy and bubbling off the course. Here was a man who was grateful for the gifts that God had bestowed upon him and who never forgot that he was privileged to have those gifts and that he was a role model for many American kids. He was a breath of fresh air in a sport that many believed had become the game of the old and the wealthy. Rickie and the likes of McIlroy were opening up the game to a new, younger audience and, indeed, giving it a new lease of life as youngsters now became encouraged to play it. This was the early legacy that he and his fellow young men bestowed on golf – they had breathed new life into the sport after the Tiger Woods era. They had made the game appear cleaner and vibrant.

It felt appropriate and timely, therefore, when Rickie came of age with that first professional win. He had already done much for the sport he adored and now he took something solid back. Sure, he was already a dollar millionaire with his winnings but this meant much more to him. It was his official entry card into the world of the best golfers: that elite club that only the few greats ever entered.

The win came on the back of those great performances at the British Open and the Bridgestone and those disappointing showings at the Barclays, the Deutsche and the BMW. The pundits had predicted that he would one day be a great but there was wild disagreement about when he would finally hit that level of consistency that would bring heady triumphs. I was of the school that firmly believed it would come when we least expected it – that, given the highs and lows, it could come at any time. Few believed, however, that it would be in just his second season as a professional.

The first win also materialised away from the glare of the PGA Tour. Having said that, winning the Korea Open at the age of twenty-two still generated masses of headlines and analysis back home in America and around the world. The tournament had been staged since 1958 and was an integral part of the OneAsia Tour – and it was hardly as if Rickie was taking on unknown players. That much was clear when his nearest rival to the crown turned out to be Rory McIlroy! Rickie closed with a three-under-par sixty-eight to finish six strokes clear of his biggest rival. He had earlier carded rounds of 67, 70 and 63 to finish 16-under-par for the tournament. The win at Woo Jeong Hills in South Korea also boosted his bank balance by a quarter of a million dollars – although the fact he had put down a marker to Rory and his other rivals meant much more than money.

Afterwards, a clearly delighted Rickie told a press conference, 'It was a lot of fun. I played well early on in the final round and then I was comfortable over the last few holes. Overall, I enjoyed the whole week. It feels great to have the first win. I played well all week, although I did have to hang in on Friday and post a score. But on Thursday, Saturday and Sunday, I had good control of my ball, I drove well and I made some putts.' Appropriately given the venue, two South Korean golfers finished third and fourth behind Rickie and Rory. Kim Meen-whee was third at ten under, and Y.E. Yang – fourth – followed at five under.

Bruce Young, expert at *iseekgolf.com*, summed up the

achievement of Rickie's win and how he had done it even with McIlroy breathing down his neck:

> That only seven players would break par for the week and yet Fowler finished 16 under gives an indication of just how much he dominated the field this week. The impressive week came a little late for him in some respects however as he missed out on a captain's selection for the USA Presidents Cup side, that place going to Bill Haas after Tiger Woods had earlier been given the nod by Captain Fred Couples. Fowler took control of the tournament with his third round of 63 and even though the world number three McIlroy produced a final round of 64 himself today he was no match for the winner.

The OneAsia Tour organisers were also happy for Rickie. They knew what this first pro win would mean to him and praised him after the event, saying how brilliantly he had played – especially as he had left McIlroy in his slipstream:

> American Rickie Fowler emphatically claimed a first career victory at the Kolon Korea Open on Sunday after storming to a six shot win over US Open champion Rory McIlroy at Woo Jeong Hills Country Club. World number 36 Fowler, 22, carded a three-under-par 68 final round to top the leader board at 16-under-par overall and complete a wire-to-wire win at the KRW1,000,000,000

OneAsia event despite finishing with back-to-back bogeys. McIlroy produced a fourth round rally after playing his final 11 holes in seven-under-par to card a superb 64, but the 22-year-old was left to rue a third round 73 as the world number three was forced to settle for a second consecutive runner-up finish.

Rickie admitted he was relieved to have finally put to bed his habit of late of starting well and fading towards the end of tournaments. He said, 'I'm happy with the way I have played on the PGA Tour, but I have never shot low enough to win. This week I played well for four rounds which I have not been able to do that in the past.'

He added that he planned to take some quality time away from the sport to plan for the next campaign and to work out an improved strategy for 2012. The maiden pro win in Korea had taken the weight off his shoulders but now he knew he would have to improve more in the following season to maintain momentum. Even in this topsy-turvy campaign in 2011, he had nonetheless managed to card the breakthrough victory and four top-ten finishes. But he was ambitious and had noted that McIlroy had gone one further with his first Major win in the same season (at the US Open). That would be a main aim for Rickie too but, in between times, the American 'Boy Wonder' was also determined to chalk up a maiden triumph on the PGA Tour.

He said, 'I am looking forward to some time off and then I can look at everything and set some goals for next year. I will play mainly on the PGA Tour next year and I would like to get my first win there, and this win will definitely help me achieve that. I also haven't made the Tour Championship in the last two years, so that is another goal for next year. But the biggest goal is to make sure I make the Ryder Cup team.'

McIlroy, to give him his due, had only praise for his conqueror in Korea. At a press conference he said, 'The damage was done during the third round with a couple of bad holes in the middle of the round. Looking back on this week, I will rue my third round, which could have been a lot better. If I had played a little better and shot a few under I might have had a chance, but Rickie has played fantastic this week and he deserves the win.'

There it was again: that admirable mutual respect for each other; the characteristics of a rivalry between the two that was fierce but nonetheless friendly.

For Rickie, the 2011 campaign had ended in glory and he really liked the taste of it. He had a relaxing holiday over the festive period, then practised hard and hit the ground running in 2012. That maiden win as a top pro had been one of the best moments of his life. Now, at the tender age of twenty-two, he had the world at his feet – or, more precisely, in his hands. And he intended to make the best of it. Rickie Fowler wanted to notch that breakthrough win on the PGA Tour as the next stage in his bid for world domination. And 2012 would see him do just that.

CHAPTER NINE

A JOB
WELLS DONE

After a relaxing holiday season at the end of 2011, in which he passed the festive season by hanging out with family and friends, Rickie welcomed in the new year with typical fervour. His resolutions were simple – he wanted to win his first PGA tournament and to win his first Major. The first wish would come true but, for the second, he would have to be patient. He had seen his good pal and biggest rival scoop his first Major in the previous year and Rickie was determined to follow Rory McIlroy's remarkable achievement. Rickie knew that he would follow in the Northern Irishman's footsteps but he also recognised that the best way to do it would be to concentrate on his own game and not put too much unnecessary pressure upon himself. Rickie had total faith in his talent and he knew he would one day secure a Major. There was no need for an inquest into his game or an overdone self-analysis: he was ever improving and he would get there when the time was right. That was enough for him; he was grounded with family and friends, who always encouraged him, and so he simply carried on playing his own game.

Of course, Rickie had won his first event as a pro in the previous season and it was his intention to build on that fine victory in the Korea Open. He had particularly enjoyed putting one over on Rory in South Korea, outplaying and out-thinking him as McIlroy rolled in six shots behind in second place. As he surveyed the sweep of tournaments for 2012, he pinpointed several that he might win – he had always done well at the Waste Management Open and the Memorial – but he decided that the best form of attack would be to simply try to hit peak form at them all and that trying to cherry-pick was a waste of time. It was undoubtedly the best option – he was no robot. Rickie knew that he would continue to have ups and downs in this new professional season. He was still a rookie, learning the ropes and trying to perfect his game with each new tournament.

His results in the early part of the PGA campaign emphasised that he remained a player with great potential – someone who would hit the heights at times but who was still striving for that all-important consistency. The first four months of 2012 saw further topsy-turvy results as Rickie worked hard to put his game together. Highlights were a tied for thirteenth finish at the Farmers Insurance Open at the end of January – his first PGA event of the new year – and a tied for seventh at the Honda Open at the beginning of April. But those positive results were mixed in with less-impressive finishes as Rickie missed the cut at the AT&T Pebble Beach National Pro-Am at the start of February and tied for forty-fifth at the Cadillac Championship the week after his fine result at the Honda, and tied for sixty-third at the Shell Houston Open in April.

There was also a tied for twenty-seventh at the first Major of the year – the 2012 Masters in Augusta – as Rickie battled for consistency. Rickie carded a 4-round 2-over-par total of 290 at the Masters, consisting of rounds of 74, 74, 72 and 70. After the first day, he said he felt much more at home at this year's tournament and that he was more comfortable with himself and with his peers. 'I'm definitely a lot more comfortable here this year. I had a great group last year, obviously, with Jason Day and Rory. We had a lot of fun and pulled off each other. This year I definitely felt a lot more comfortable and a lot more at home.'

Rickie also showed how mentally stronger he was becoming when he was asked how he felt about some players and fans having fun at his expense because he was not clean-cut like most pro golfers. In his reply, Rickie showed his self-confidence and stubbornness as he more or less said he didn't give a damn what others thought of him! 'Obviously with the facial hair and the moustache and stuff, it's kind of all for fun and just showing off my personality. There's a lot of people that don't like it, and that's one of the main reasons it's still around – just showing that I'm myself and I'm not trying to be like anyone else. Maybe it's a good lesson to some kids out there – don't worry about what others think of you, just be yourself.'

Rickie was clearly getting in his stride with fighting talk like that! He was his own man and he would live as he wanted and grace the golf courses on the circuit as he wanted. He would answer to no one but himself. It was strong stuff from a youngster only just settling into the PGA circuit and a sign that the boy was growing up and felt secure and self-confident. With that proud, unflinching state of mind, it would surely not be long before he achieved that main New Year resolution and won his first PGA tournament? He was growing into a golfer and a person of stature and determination with each passing event – and the maiden win would come soon enough.

At the end of April, Rickie finished tied for tenth in the prestigious Zurich Classic of New Orleans with a 13-under-par total of 275. That included rounds of 71, 69 and 70 but it was his brilliant second round of 65 that suggested all his hard work was paying off and that, if he could just repeat that sort of form for four rounds, victory would be his at some tournament soon. Rickie admitted to the press after that awesome round, 'I am pleased with the way I am playing. I feel good where my game is at. It was nice to make a few par putts early on to keep the momentum going and I did hit some good iron shots. It felt good to shoot a low round and put myself in a good position.'

It was what he had been working towards after his win in the Korea Open. Rickie felt confident that success in the PGA would come for sure if he kept his head down and that was now the case. That sixty-five in Avondale, Louisiana, was arguably one of the most important rounds of his career –

it provided the launch pad for his wonderful performance at the next tournament on the PGA list: that all-important maiden PGA victory as he triumphed at the Wells Fargo Championship at the beginning of May 2012.

Rickie arrived early at the Quail Hollow Course in Charlotte, North Carolina, to prepare for his assault on the title. He practised hard but remained calm and collected: he was determined and focused on the prize. He knew more than anyone that to get the monkey off his back would need a total golfing effort – especially as McIlroy and Darren Points had also both turned up at the course intent on walking off with the $1 million cheque. In the end, it would need even more concentration and channelled intent as Rickie was forced into a play-off for the crown with the other two golfers.

It probably shouldn't have needed a play-off – Rickie had started with a sizzling first round of sixty-six and McIlroy could only manage seventy. But Rickie seemed to have lost it with a disappointing second-round score of seventy-two – the worst of him, McIlroy and Points in the contest. Set against that, Rickie also carded a third-round sixty-seven and a final-round sixty-nine. All three men finished on a 274 total of 14-under-par and headed for the unenviable pressure of the play-off. Experienced and novices alike have been known to falter in the sweat and stress of a play-off but this was the day when Rickie Fowler came of age. It was the day where he got the better of arch-rival McIlroy and the unexpected challenge of journeyman Points. It was the day that Rickie proved he could handle the pressure, that he was good enough to win on the PGA Tour and that he could live with the ever burgeoning talent of McIlroy.

ESPN best summed up the wonder of Rickie's victory – and the indelible imprint he had left on the sport with his flashy colours and love of excitement – on Sunday, 6 May 2012, saying:

> The thrill-seeking passion for motocross as a teenager. The head-turning clothing he brought to the PGA Tour as a rookie, such as the bright orange ensemble from head-to-toe on Sundays. With a chance to finally breakthrough for his first PGA Tour win, the kid showed his true colors.
>
> In a three-way play-off that featured U.S. Open champion Rory McIlroy, the 23-year-old Fowler gambled with a 51-degree wedge that had to be perfect on an 18th hole at Quail Hollow that had yielded only four birdies all day. And it was. Fowler stuffed his shot into 4 feet for a birdie on the first extra hole to beat McIlroy and D.A. Points and win the Wells Fargo Championship on Sunday.

Note the word 'gambled' in that report. Yes, even when everything he had worked for was at stake on the play-off, Rickie refused to try to graft his way to victory. The boy had to do it in colour and in style – he wanted the win badly but was prepared to gamble the lot to win the trophy in a typically dramatic and memorable fashion. It was a defining moment in his career and one the fans at the course and watching at home on TV would not easily forget.

Finally, America's golfing wunderkind had beat his hoodoo and won a big PGA event. He was on his way to world fame and fortune. He now became the golfer the kids wanted to be and the golfer the veteran fans wanted to see. After Tiger's implosion, Fowler brought hope and a renewed innocence and vitality to the sport. He helped put America back on the golfing map with his natural ability to achieve results – and do it entertainingly. Rickie admitted as much at the post-tournament press conference. He said, 'I didn't want to play it safe. I had a good number [133 yards] and I was aiming right of the hole with the wind coming out of the right and, if I hit a perfect shot, it comes down right on the stick … I hit a perfect shot at the right time and I was going for it.'

They say fortune favours the brave and that was certainly a mantra that Rickie Fowler lived by and was willing to fail or succeed by. Fans flocked to watch him as his fame spread, precisely because they knew he would be colourful, passionate and sometimes off-the-wall in his approach and delivery. Rickie had brought some fun and joy back to American golf: he was a beacon of light after the dark days of Tiger Woods's very public marriage break-up and subsequent golfing demise. Woods would, of course, eventually return to form and play top-notch golf once again but, during that fallout period, it was the likes of Fowler and his fellow PGA novices with their inherent decency and good sportsmanship that captured the imagination of the American public.

Rickie had felt he would have a good chance of success at the Wells Fargo from the moment he arrived, right through to his eventual victory. He had played the course on two previous occasions, finishing with a top-ten and a top-twenty spot. After his first-round sixty-six, he said, 'I've played well here, had one good finish here along with another one that was OK and this is a course that I like. I enjoy playing here. It's usually in great shape and it looks like we're going to have warm, good weather for the week.

'It's a fun course. I feel like I'm comfortable off the tee here and I seem to hit a lot of good iron shots here.'

Rickie was asked how he felt playing against the other younger players, like McIlroy, who lived near him and whom he was now measuring his progress against. His reply summed up his determination and drive to win, especially against those of his own generation: 'I hate to lose and I definitely don't want to. When you're playing against other young guys around your age, they're the guys you don't want to lose to the most. It's definitely a friendly rivalry. It's not like we dislike each other or anything like that. But it's always fun to beat each other and, when you're behind them, you're trying to catch back up and put them behind you.'

At a press conference before the tournament it was put to Rickie that he hadn't won anything yet, unlike Rory. 'I won in Korea!' he exclaimed. 'And I beat Rory!'

He also said he 'wouldn't be surprised if a win was just around the corner,' adding, 'It's tough to put seventy-two holes of great golf together. But the last couple weeks I've been hitting the ball well and putting myself in a good position.

'I definitely feel like the amount of people expecting or

thinking that I can win is a compliment. That is my main goal for this year; that's my main focus.'

And after his second round was completed, Rickie once again seemed to suggest that this was a tournament that he could win come Sunday. He said, 'This is one of the best events we play all year here at Quail Hollow. We've got a pretty packed leader board so I'm just going to try to put myself into position coming down to the last nine, maybe six holes tomorrow and give it a shot and see what happens. It would be nice to be on the top of it.'

And it was nice because that is exactly where he did finish at the end of the tournament: on top of it, the 2012 champion of the Wells Fargo Championship. After that dramatic play-off triumph in which he held his nerve against McIlroy and Points, Rickie had the look of a balloon that had just been popped. He was delighted, of course, but also relieved and the energy clearly seeped from him after that adrenaline-pumping finale had taken so much out of him. He told the post-event press conference, 'It'll take a bit for it to sink in. Obviously, there [are] a lot of people that have helped me out through the years and going through and thanking them one by one is going to take a bit. I've already thought of a few and it was nice to have my mom and my girlfriend here. My dad is still probably jumping around at home – he's probably one of the most excited of all of us.'

Could Rickie put his finger on exactly how he had moved up from contender to winner? Had he been working on anything special to improve his game? 'I've been hitting the ball well and swinging it well and I feel like, mentally,

I've been doing all the right things,' he said. 'But the biggest improvement has been course management and patience, staying focused throughout rounds and not letting bogeys and doubles get the best of me. Also, moving on and making the most out of the bad rounds, like I did on Friday, and focusing on putting together a good week.'

Rickie was also asked at the press conference if he had imagined he would be winning on the PGA circuit so soon after leaving college. Had his results before the win made him believe he would scoop a Major sooner rather than later? He replied:

I put up a fight pretty early [in his career], got into a play-off at Fry's my second event out. So I knew I could be in contention and I knew that I could win out here. It was just a case of putting it all together – whether it be four rounds or being in the right position at the right time. But I knew it was going to be tough. Taking the step from junior golf to college golf – or to amateur golf and the PGA Tour – is the biggest leap you take. These are the best players in the world. It's not easy to win out here, so it's nice to have the first one out of the way.

Despite the constant pressure and public exposure, Rickie had always struck me as a young man who rarely got flustered. He appeared remarkably calm on the outside and often used the word 'fun' to describe his work on the golf course, which suggested he enjoyed even the most stressful rounds, rather than endured them. He was someone who always had a smile, someone who was always willing to sign an autograph for an appreciative fan and someone who never bad-mouthed his opponents. He was a naturally nice guy as well as a young golfer who was well on his way to becoming a golfing legend.

Rickie conceded that he did sometimes suffer from the butterflies in the stomach but added that, generally, he was as cool and calm inside as he looked on the outside. Obviously, he was more emotional than usual after chalking up his first win – and because his mother and girlfriend were in attendance. And there was the added emotional aspect of winning without his erstwhile coach Barry McDonnell, the brilliant swing coach he had worked with since he was a boy. Barry had died aged seventy-five in May 2011, due to complications after he suffered a heart attack.

Rickie's dad Rod had explained just how close his son and Barry became over the years. 'He was just a one-of-a-kind guy, old school like Ben Hogan and Bobby Jones,' Rod told *The Press-Enterprise*. 'Barry passed on a lot of great stuff to all of our kids in the community. There's not a lot of coaches like him around.' Rod added that Rickie was just five when he wanted to begin taking lessons but that Barry made him wait until he was seven.

Bill Teasdale, Barry's best friend, would reminisce after his death on the relationship between Rickie and Barry, saying the duo had a special bond after all those years working together. 'I remember Mike McGraw, the coach at Oklahoma State, said to me, "Well, what does Barry tell him?" I told him, "They don't say anything to each other, they just sit and nod at each other and every now and then, someone says, 'I like that.'" They understood each other without talking to each other. There was some magic there.'

Indeed, there was. And that helped explain why Rickie became choked up after his win. He had his loved ones with him but Barry could not be there. Rickie paid tribute to him after the win, explaining that, when he did get emotional, he attempted not to show it in public but that the loss of Barry had made that impossible on this occasion. 'I try to hold it in as much as I can,' he said. 'It's definitely a lot of emotion. It's a lot of fun winning. But I tried not to mention my swing coach Barry a whole lot because that definitely pulls a whole lot out of me. It's nice to have him watching down.'

Rory McIlroy was the first to congratulate Rickie on his brilliant win and Rory said it hadn't surprised him in the least. 'I think it was just a matter of time before he won. It seems like this tournament produces first-time winners – Anthony Kim, myself and now Rickie. It's great to see. He probably has gone through a little bit of scrutiny and a lot of pressure trying to get that first win. But now that win is out of the way, the pressure on him will hopefully ease a little.'

Rory was also impressed by how Rickie had kept his nerve to win at the eighteenth and how he had achieved that final winning birdie, saying, 'He deserved to win after he played the hole the way he did. It wasn't a birdie hole.'

The young American was also hugged by his mum Lynne and his girlfriend Alexandra. Lynne told the Associated Press she was as relieved as her own son that he had finally got the monkey off his back with this maiden triumph, adding, 'I'm over the top. I'm relieved for him because this is an expectation from the people, the fans and the tournament directors. Now he can hopefully carry on and do the work that he likes to do.'

Rickie's first PGA Tour win was also celebrated by his old college, Oklahoma State. The Rivals Cup – which promotes the collegiate affiliations of professional athletes by ranking their achievements in professional sports – made sure of that on their website. They stated, 'They say the rich get richer, and that statement couldn't be more true in the Rivals Cup on the PGA Tour. Rickie Fowler's win in Charlotte on Sunday was the first of his professional career on the PGA Tour, but the third win for Oklahoma State in 2012. Fowler's win opens up a huge lead for former Cowboys in the professional game and clearly establishes the OSU men's golf program as the one having the greatest impact at the game's highest level.'

That must have pleased Rickie – he always stressed his college links and how key Oklahoma State had been in his development. He would, no doubt, also have been tickled by the description the Rivals Cup website offered up about his fans mimicking his fashion sense! The website added, 'I was lucky enough to be in attendance Sunday at Quail Hollow and I can tell you that Rickie's win was extremely well received. At least that's what any 1 of the 5,000 or so kids in flat-brimmed orange Puma hats would tell you. The Quail Hollow membership you ask? Maybe not so much, but that's just my own observation.'

Rickie packed his bags and headed off triumphant into

the night with his mum and his girlfriend. He had finally achieved his dream of winning on the PGA Tour in just his third season as a member. He enjoyed a slap-up dinner and fun and laughter the next day with his family and then unwound and relaxed for a couple of days.

Then it was back to work and the next stop on the journey was Miami for The Players Championship at Ponte Vedra Beach. Rickie believed he could continue his fine form at the event and he would be proved absolutely right in that respect. He was ambitious and had the determination and sheer brilliance to go right to the very top: he was sure of that.

He may have won on the PGA but this was definitely no time to be sitting on his laurels: the first part of his mission for world domination had been completed but now he would set his sights on the next piece of an evolving jigsaw. Yes, he wanted to win a Major as his pal and closest rival McIlroy had done. The first win on the PGA Tour had whetted his appetite. He very much liked the feeling winning had brought and how it had made his loved ones so delighted and proud too. Just imagine how he and they would feel and react when he put a Major to bed. The hard work hadn't finished after the Wells Fargo victory: it had only just begun.

CHAPTER TEN

MAN OF
THE PEOPLE

After the euphoria and sheer joy of that Wells Fargo win, Rickie headed for Florida the following Thursday determined that he would build on that quality maiden PGA Tour victory. He had the momentum and the plan was simple: keep it going and, hopefully, chalk up another big win at the prestigious Players Championship. In the event, he would not manage that, but he came agonisingly close to doing so. Rickie finished as one of four runners-up to eventual champion Matt Kuchar at the Tournament Players Club (more generally known as the TPC) at Sawgrass.

The venue is also the HQ of the PGA Tour and so has a special aura for the golfers who tread its hallowed turf – after all, who wouldn't want to win at the home of American golf? It is similar to football in England – playing and winning at Wembley holds a particular reverence for players. To win at

Wembley in a cup final or in an England match has a special place in any English player's heart. So it is with the TPC – win there and you win in front of the big chiefs of American golf!

Rickie arrived early to practise and said he felt good. The weather was usually good and the course immaculate – almost like velvet green it was so smooth. The importance of the course to the sport can be gauged by the fact that it featured for many years on the bestselling Tiger Woods PGA Tour video games. And Rickie revelled in the attention given to him after his first PGA win. He was asked at a press conference how it felt to be arriving at a tournament after that maiden win on the Tour and whether it was a load off his back. He said:

> Well, it's nice to come off a win. That's something I've been working on for a couple years now and obviously there's been a lot of expectation, both from the media side and my side. It's nice to finally get the first one out of the way. It was nice to get down here Sunday night. I took yesterday off and went out and played a few holes this morning.
>
> I think the first one [win] is definitely the hardest. You're either a PGA Tour winner or you're not. Now I'm looking forward to getting back in contention and working on my second [win].

Yet Rickie would get off to a disappointing start, carding a seventy-two, which left him well outside the early pacesetters.

Brits Martin Laird and Ian Poulter led after the first round, both shooting seven-under-par sixty-fives. Blake Adams led the USA's charge, one point behind the dynamic duo in third place. But Rickie gradually reduced the deficit with a sixty-nine on the Friday, a brilliant sixty-six on the Saturday and a sound enough seventy on the Sunday. That left him with a final score of 277, which was 11-under-par and good enough to earn him a tied for second place. Coming after the win at the Wells Fargo, it served to reinforce his growing reputation as a serious contender on the PGA Tour.

The bubbly boy from OSU was winning a reputation for fine, adventurous golf as well as being friendly and approachable. There were no airs or graces with Rickie Fowler; none of the arrogance and 'I'm a superstar, don't bother me' unpleasantness that defined some others in the sport. Rickie remained the same likeable lad he was at OSU and that he was determined to remain, however successful he was in the golfing strata. In his eyes, he owed the fans for their devotion to the sport and would always have time for them. They were part of his success story and nothing would change that: he would ensure he always had time to sign an autograph and have a quick chat. He had no desire to become aloof; he loved his fans and appreciated them.

It was on the Saturday at the TPC when he finally arrived in the top section of the leader board. At the end of play, he was third behind the leader Kevin Na and Matt Kuchar, both fellow Americans, with a 9-under-par total of 207. At the end of play on the Sunday, Kuchar had claimed the crown and a cheque for $1,710,000. Rickie and his three fellow runners-up walked away with $627,000 apiece – not bad for four days' work, especially when it came on the back of the $1,170,000 Rickie earned for his Wells Fargo breakthrough. His bank manager was no doubt delighted with how he was going about his work!

Rickie, however, was more concerned with the glory than the money. Of course, he enjoyed the financial rewards and the gilded lifestyle they afforded him but he remained ever the perfectionist – the boy who loved golf for the 'fun' it offered him but also the boy who wanted to make winning a habit. So it was that he was, perhaps, a little tough on himself after finishing tied for second in the Players. There was a feeling that, with a little more focus, Rickie could actually have won at the TPC. At the final hole, he had a chance of a birdie, which would have put him within a stroke of Kuchar, but his putt came to a halt at the right of the hole, condemning him to the runner-up spot.

Golfweek made the valid point that Rickie could have put more pressure on Kuchar but for that setback at the final hole; that where Rickie had struggled to make that birdie at the eighteenth, Kuchar had been consistent in pushing on steadily. They continued: 'Kuchar avoided the big mistakes that slowed so many other contenders – starting with Kevin Na – and kept out of the water on the TPC Sawgrass at the end.'

Golf.com wrote that Rickie had left Kuchar with an inevitable triumph after blowing the birdie:

His [Kuchar's] lead was back to two strokes and Fowler, who had hit it close on 18, was trying to close with three straight birdies. But he missed his seven-foot birdie putt to the right, after watching Curtis roll in a birdie on exactly the same line, and Fowler's miss gave Kuchar some breathing room he was glad to have. All he needed for the win was a bogey at the 72nd hole. When he ran a 6-iron shot onto the front third of the green, he had three putts to win. He got down in two, and then he picked up two. His young sons ran onto the green and he hoisted them to his chest like shining trophies.

The comment about Kuchar lifting his sons like 'shining trophies' was a nice angle and few would begrudge him his moment of triumph. This would remain Kuchar's biggest success on the circuit and he was a well-liked and popular figure. Some pundits dubbed him 'a plodder' but not his fellow players. Rickie was one of the first to congratulate him and shake his hand after this phenomenal win, with equally phenomenal prize money.

Of course, Rickie did not need it spelling out that he could have done even better at the TPC. He remained his own strongest critic but also, as we have noted earlier, liked to see the positives, rather than getting bogged down with negatives. After all, he had now finished first and second in his last two tournaments and that was something to be proud of. He admitted as much at the post-tournament press conference: 'Yeah, it was a very successful week for me, coming off the win and finishing second here when I have not made a cut here before. It was a lot of fun to be in contention and I tried to give it a run there at the end. But Kuch played very well today, very solid, and I just fell a couple of shots short.'

Rickie was asked what he felt had changed in his game that had led to this run of success. He replied that he had been working hard on his game and that it was finally all coming together:

I'm swinging it well and I have a lot of confidence in myself and my game now. I feel like I'm managing myself around the golf course and throughout tournaments better and getting myself in the right positions.

The first day I went out there I shot even par, which obviously is not the greatest start. But I hung on in and got back in contention. I feel I've missed too many cuts in previous years because of not being patient and sticking it out, staying focused and trying to get the most out of every round. So during the past few weeks I've been very patient, played very well and had a lot of confidence in my game. I've felt calm and confident coming down the stretch when the nerves are supposed to be worst. I've been ready to go for it.

Kuchar was full of praise for Rickie and the sustained challenge he made to try to rein him in. He was particularly impressed by Rickie's 20-foot birdie putt on the seventeenth, which drew him to within two shots of the leader. Kuchar answered that with his own brilliant putt on the sixteenth after he had watched Rickie pump his fist in delight at his putt on the seventeenth! Kuchar said, 'I saw Rickie's putt; watched the thing disappear and he gave a big fist pump. I knew it got him to within two shots and he could birdie eighteen to bring it within one. That could have changed the whole scenario of how I would have approached and played eighteen. So I was really excited to drop that birdie on sixteen. That was big.'

Kuchar had lit up the weekend with his constant smile and clear humility when he did finally clinch the winner's trophy and cheque. Like Rickie, he is a natural nice guy but he had waited many a moon to notch up a win as big as this one at The Players Championship. Afterwards, Kuchar congratulated Rickie for pushing him so hard and explained his own golfing philosophy, which didn't sound a million miles away from Rickie's own views on the game. Just as Rickie insists on 'having fun' at every tournament he competes in, so Kuchar said it was important to him that he enjoyed playing. Kuchar said:

I love playing the game of golf. I have fun doing it. I'm a golf junkie. I have to force myself to take vacations where I cannot play golf because the game is just always so challenging. And I think it's that challenge that's addictive to me. The smile is there because I'm having a good time. Now, granted, if I'm shooting ten-over par, you're probably not going to see me real happy. I'm hopefully going to behave myself appropriately, thanks to my mother, but I'm not going to be near as happy as when I'm making birdies. It was such an amazing feeling to win here – playing among the game's best, to come out on top, to do it on Mother's Day… it really is magical.

Kuchar was a worthy winner and Rickie would be the first man to say that. But Rickie hadn't done too badly himself of late with that triumph at the Wells Fargo and his runner-up spot at The Players Championship. He said he now planned to take a well-earned few days off, away from golf, and would just hang out with friends and 'have fun'. Then it would be back to work and a run of six big tournaments on the trot.

First up was the Crowne Plaza Invitational at Colonial and Rickie's fine form continued as he ended up tied for fifth place thanks to a 5-under-par total of 275. For many events in 2012 Rickie had tended to start slowly and build momentum in the final two days. The Wells Fargo win had been something of an anomaly in that he started well, struggled a little and finished well. But at the Crowne Plaza he turned everything on its head by starting well, continuing well and finishing well. It was just the latest example of how much more confident and how much more consistently good he was becoming as he matured as a pro golfer. Each new tournament brought a new experience and Rickie was learning how to deal with different courses, different climates and different challenges set by his closest rivals.

He always looked forward to the Crowne Plaza at Fort Worth in Texas. Rickie liked the state, he liked the course and he liked the fact that he was paired with a likeable older guy for the opening round: Jason Dufner. He also liked the conditions he and the other golfers faced: it was usually hot but with a gusty wind to accompany. It was challenging and Rickie had always loved taking on challenges and defeating them. The tournament is an invitational reserved for 120 golfers but Fulton Allem, Keith Clearwater and Corey Pavin joined the lucky 120 after receiving special exemptions as past champions pre-2000. So Rickie was up against testing conditions and testing rivals. But he gave a good account of himself by coming in the top 5 with rounds of 68, 68, 70 and 69.

Zach Johnson was the eventual winner by one stroke, ahead of Rickie's playing partner Dufner. Rickie declared himself pleased with his four days' work and said he was happy to have finished in the top five of another big event. Next up, at the start of June 2012, was the Memorial at Muirfield in Dublin, Ohio. This was usually viewed as an ideal warm-up for the US Open but, as such, it was not what Rickie had been hoping for as he struggled round the course to finish in the fifty-second spot. It would be a blast from the past who stole the headlines – yes, the return to winning form of Tiger Woods. The Tiger's fifth win at the Memorial meant he had now tied with tournament host Jack Nicklaus for second place on the career-victories list with seventy-three victories, trailing only behind Sam Snead (eighty-two).

Woods admitted the win had given him a boost ahead of the US Open, which would take place eleven days later. He said, 'It's special for me to reach seventy-three wins here, to do it with Jack here, with his involvement in the tournament and the game.'

For Rickie, there would be no such glory. He admitted that he had underperformed and that it had been a disappointment in terms of preparation for the US Open. His demeanour certainly changed from the start to the end of the tournament. Before the opening round, he had been optimistic about his chances and looking forward to making a statement, as he had finished runner-up two years previously. Rickie had said, 'I am looking forward to this week. I've played really well here before. Last year I made a lot of birdies and ended up making too many others and bogeys. So two years ago I gave it a run and ended up finishing second. Hopefully we can eliminate some of the bogeys this week and get up there on top.' But after it was all over, he sounded flat, as if he were tired and needed a good rest. He said, 'Today was one of those days. Out here, if you don't hit your number perfectly, within one or two paces, you're either in the bunker with a tough up-and-down or long on a down slope out of the rough and you're not getting up and down. Going to get a lot of Sundays from now on, some good ones and some bad ones, and this is not going to be the last bad one.'

Rickie's next slice of competitive action, a couple of weeks later, was at the US Open in San Francisco and it would be another 'bad one'. Once again Rickie finished far down the field, coming home at tied for forty-first, with four rounds in the seventies. Instead, it was Webb Simpson who was showing off the winner's trophy. His final round of sixty-eight meant he beat Graeme McDowell and Michael Thompson by one shot. For Rickie, there was only despondency. He had said previously that the course demanded you be at your best to win but he struggled to find a decent range and it was soon clear that he was not going to be a realistic contender for the title.

At least he had the consolation of knowing he would soon have a chance to put things right, for next up was the British Open – a tournament in which he already had fond memories – and he always enjoyed visiting the UK for individual and team events. The previous year, of course, he had tied for fifth at Sandwich in Kent but now he once again found it difficult to make a lasting impact as he battled for consistency at Lytham St Annes, near Blackpool on the northwest coast of England.

Before his opening tee-off, Rickie had certainly sounded confident enough and in good spirits, saying, 'I'm really looking forward to the tournament. As far as Majors go, the Open Championship has been definitely my best performance over the last two years. I finished tied for fourteenth at St Andrews and tied for fifth last year. The course is in great shape. It's a tough driving course – very narrow – and there's a lot more rough than I've seen the last couple years at Open Championships. But I'm looking forward to the week.'

However, his dip in form would show no sign of abating at Lytham St Annes. Again, he was stuck with four rounds in the 70s and ended up with a card of 283, which was 3-over-par and left him tied for thirty-first. Yet he did not sound down in the dumps when he was asked how he had enjoyed the event. He said he had enjoyed the tournament, although conditions had not been easy with a 'blowing wind.' When asked what he would take away from his week, he replied, 'I just love playing over here. I love links golf. I love the way it sets up for my game. I love playing in the wind, getting to hit different shots on the ground or in the air. Just a lot of fun over here so I enjoy it. Like last year, I had a chance but this week I just didn't get off to the start I wanted and made a few too many mistakes.'

At least he had the consolation that his failings at Lytham were not on the scale of those of his pal Adam Scott. The Aussie spectacularly lost the plot on the final round after his earlier work had propelled him to what appeared certain victory. Going into the final day, he led by four strokes and was six ahead of eventual winner Ernie Els. But Scott turned victory into defeat as he bogeyed the last four holes and South African Els confirmed his unexpected triumph as he birdied the eighteenth to finish one shot ahead on the final leader board. It was a capitulation to match McIlroy's defeat at the Masters a year earlier. But, like Rickie Fowler, Scott showed an optimistic side to his approach that singled him out as a good loser with a good attitude. Even after that downfall, Scott said, 'I'm very disappointed but I played so beautifully for most of the week, I really shouldn't let this bring me down. I know I've let a really great chance slip through my fingers today but somehow I'll look back and take the positives from it.'

But worse was to come for Rickie as he tried desperately to regain his momentum at the final Major of 2012: the US PGA Championship. He joined the world's best golfers as they gathered at Kiawah Island in South Carolina but there was not the usual air of electric anticipation – it was as if the event did not have the import that it usually radiated. Many pundits put this down to the tournament suffering in the shadow of the wonderful London Olympics, which were making headline news across the world and still had a full week to run as the US PGA teed off. The BBC's golf correspondent Conor McNamara summed up this unusual state of affairs by saying, 'The US PGA Championship gets under way on Thursday at Kiawah Island in South Carolina – the venue of the infamous "War on the Shore" Ryder Cup battle between the United States and Europe in 1991, where the USA came out on top. But with London 2012 dominating the sporting agenda, golf finds itself far from the centre of attention.'

Rickie struggled more than most to get into his normal game and ended up missing the cut, much to his and his many fans' dismay. To make matters worse, McIlroy, the young man Rickie liked to compare himself with at the biggest events, finished victorious – his second Major, after the US Open, within the space of just over a year. As if that wasn't bad enough, the official PGA website then proceeded to rub salt into the wound for Rickie with a glowing salute to Rory's achievement. They said:

Right down to his red shirt, Rory McIlroy looked every bit the part of golf's next star in another command performance at the PGA Championship. McIlroy validated his record-setting U.S. Open win last year by blowing away the field Sunday at Kiawah Island. One last birdie from 25 feet on the 18th hole gave him a 6-under 66 for an eight-shot victory, breaking the PGA Championship record for margin of victory that Jack Nicklaus set in 1980. The 23-year-old from Northern Ireland returned to No. 1 in the world, and he became the youngest player since Seve Ballesteros to win two Majors. Tiger Woods was about four months older than McIlroy when he won his second major. Just like the U.S. Open, this one was never seriously in doubt.

Rory was buzzing afterwards, saying, 'It was a great round of golf. I'm speechless. It's just been incredible. I had a good feeling about it at the start. But I never imagined to do this.' Rickie was down but not out; of course, he was disappointed at his own showing but he still had the magnanimity to congratulate his rival and to praise him for a remarkable achievement. Rickie's tournament had ended after he could only card a seventy-four and an eighty in the windy conditions that also affected the games of other big names.

Above left: Even as a teenager, Rickie cut a confident and assured figure on the green.

© *David Cannon/Getty Images*

Above right: Rickie and home-country hero Rory McIlroy in earnest competition for the coveted 'Worst Dressed Award' at the 2007 Walker Cup in Northern Ireland.

© *Peter Muhly/AFP/Getty Images*

Below: A fresh-faced Fowler celebrates the USA's win at the same tournament.

© *David Cannon/Getty Images*

Above: Rickie has become known worldwide for his unique, eye-catching outfits.

© *Sam Greenwood/Getty Images*

Below: Getting into the Chinese spirit with Justin Rose at the historic Bund waterfront of Shanghai.

© *Johannes Eisele/AFP/Getty Images*

Above: Posing in trademark orange with his mother and girlfriend Alexandra Brown after the 2012 Wells Fargo Championship.   © *Streeter Lecka/Getty Images*

Below left: A sun-tanned, black-clad Rickie Fowler tees off the 14th hole in scorching heat at the Abu Dhabi 2015 Championships.   © *Francois Nel/Getty Images*

Below right: Europe's Justin Rose enjoys a closer look at Rickie's radical 'USA' head-shave before battle for the 2014 Ryder Cup commences.

© *David Cannon/Getty Images*

Above: Any excuse: old rivals Rickie and Rory McIlroy race to be the first to whip up the perfect Bloody Mary in Abu Dhabi. © *Ross Kinnaird/Getty Images*

Below: Rickie and Spanish favourite Sergio Garcia stand by as Rory McIlroy hoists his long-awaited Open trophy. One thing is for sure: more epic battles between the two are in store. © *David Cannon/Getty Images*

The likes of Sergio Garcia, Webb Simpson, Jason Day, Hunter Mahan and Angel Cabrera also failed to make the cut. But that was scant consolation for Rickie and the trouble he encountered at the event can be gauged by the poor quality of his second-round eighty. It consisted of three bogeys, one double-bogey and one triple-bogey.

There was more bad news for Rickie when the American squad for the 2012 Ryder Cup at Medinah near Chicago was announced and he failed to make it. Most pundits were shocked by the decision of US skipper Davis Love III's decision. European Ryder Cup player Martin Kaymer found it hard to understand why rookie Brandt Snedeker had been chosen instead of Rickie or Hunter Mahan. Love III had chosen Dustin Johnson, Steve Stricker, Jim Furyk and Snedeker to join the eight automatic qualifiers in his twelve-man team. That led Kaymer to say, 'I expected Dustin and Stricker but also thought Rickie had a good chance because he made a really good impression in Wales two years ago. It was a tough decision between Snedeker, Hunter Mahan and Rickie Fowler. You could have put those three names in a hat and picked any one of them.'

Rickie was obviously disappointed not to have made the team and he certainly had some justification in feeling that way. He had, after all, been one of the success stories of the American team back in 2010 at Celtic Manor when he was just twenty-one, establishing himself as the youngest-ever American Ryder Cup player. And in 2012 he had won his first PGA tournament at the Wells Fargo and finished runner-up at The Players Championship, as well as achieving a tie for fifth at the Crowne Plaza Invitational. It appeared that Love III was worried about Rickie's more recent form though, including missing the cut at the US PGA Championship. The theme of inconsistency – which we have debated at length in this chapter – was picked up by a number of golfing experts. 'Back in 2010, Fowler was selected to his first Ryder Cup team … his 2010 experience wasn't without its blemishes and controversies, but he has experience, and he's shown flashes of brilliance this season that indicate he could've been an asset,' said the *Bleacher Report*. 'Fowler won the Wells Fargo in a play-off in May, and he followed that up with a tie for second in The Players Championship, as well as a tie for fifth at the Crowne Plaza Invitational. It's clear that inconsistency is one thing that kept Fowler off this team – that, and his recent play. He hasn't registered a top-10 finish since the Crowne Plaza Invitational, and he missed the cut at the PGA Championship less than a month ago.'

Golfchannel.com was also surprised that Rickie had been left out. Before the squad announcement, they offered up cases for him to be included and were ignored. The case for his inclusion summed up brilliantly the opinion of most pundits, including myself:

He's young, he's hip, he's cool. For an organization like the PGA of America, which is constantly trying to grow the game and also coincidentally runs the Ryder Cup, including Fowler means an entire generation of flat-billed teeny-boppers may be eyeballing this biennial competition for the very first time. More importantly, Fowler is a glue guy. He may not be the best ball-striker nor putter in the world, but he's hardly the worst at either. And as a good-natured, likable player, he can easily be paired with any of the 11 other players on the roster, giving Love plenty of options on where to play him over the first two days.

Typically, Rickie would refuse to criticise Love III for his decision, instead focusing on his own loss of form and admitting that he hadn't necessarily expected to get the nod because of his current run of inconsistent results. Once again, he was choosing not to walk down that pessimistic way of thinking and acting out. When questioned by the press on his omission at the BMW International a couple of weeks before the Ryder Cup, he said, 'With the way I played in the last two weeks, I definitely felt like I was on the outside looking in. I knew that, if I was going to be picked, it would not be down to my recent play but my play earlier this year. But he obviously went with some guys who are playing well right now, which I completely understand.'

And when quizzed on how he felt about his close pal Hunter Mahan also missing out, he added, 'It [making the team] was a main goal going into this year for us both. With Hunter just missing out on points, it's a tough position to be in. We both didn't play as well as we would have liked to in the last couple weeks and it seems like Davis definitely went for the two guys that were playing well. And with the other two spots being the veteran picks, it just happened to be Hunter and I who were left out.'

They were generous words; words that showed how big a man this boy had become. No sign of recriminations or bitterness – just an acceptance that this wasn't going to be his moment and an understanding of why Love III had chosen not to take him and Mahan to Medinah.

In the event, Rickie and Hunter may even have viewed the decision as a blessing. Of course, he would undoubtedly rather have gone into the record books as one of the American stars on show during the tournament in September of 2012 but he wouldn't have enjoyed being tarred with the brush of failure for the second successive time, as Europe won yet again. The Americans gave an improved performance after Celtic Manor but they still could not get the better of their European counterparts and this time the defeat was on home soil. Ironically, after Rickie's pre-tournament surprise that he had been omitted from the team, it was Martin Kaymer who helped seal America's defeat by making a putt on the eighteenth hole, ensuring that Europe would, at least, retain the trophy. And when Tiger Woods bogeyed on the final green, victory was assured for the Europeans, who had needed to complete a remarkable comeback, since they looked certain to be defeated as the match entered its final day.

Rickie had hoped to use the BMW Championship to get back on track after his disappointing second half to the season. It might also have been helpful to help him shake off the blues after his omission from the American Ryder Cup squad. There were hints that he might be improving in the event at Carmel in Indiana but the same old worrying inconsistencies also raised their ugly heads as he failed to build on momentum and finished tied for forty-first.

Those efforts may have boosted Rickie's bank balance by $30,000 but that was small change in terms of what he really wanted – to break out of the stranglehold of dismal finishes that was driving him crazy in a season that had also seen him win his first PGA tournament. He was asked by the press what he had pinpointed as being the cause of his troubles. As usual, he answered with honesty: 'I've actually been striking the ball well, starting putts on line, but I just haven't been getting the ball in the hole quick enough and have had a few penalty shots. I struggle at getting off to good starts. I'm over par early so seem to be fighting back all day every day. But overall it's been a great year.'

Being Rickie, he still managed to see a positive side to things. He loved the way his famed army of fans turned up to watch him play and felt that one good thing right now was that he was hopefully proving to be a good role model for them, with his manners, his civilised attitude to the golfers he came up against and the way he was determined to move forward by working hard and putting in the hours of hard practice. He said, 'It's a lot of fun for me to go week to week, city to city, and receive the same support. I have a great following, a great group of fans, and it's good seeing the ones that are on the younger side who are looking for me to be a positive role model. Hopefully their parents are allowing them to look up to me. I want to be a good role model and to play good golf.'

And the result hadn't been all that bad – his finish meant he had confirmed his debut at the prestigious Tour Championship a couple of weeks later. As *Golfchannel. com* pointed out: 'Fowler closed clumsily at the BMW Championship with a 2-over-par 74, but it was good enough to hold onto his top-30 spot in FedExCup points and advance to East Lake in Atlanta.'

Rickie did manage to make inroads on his topsy-turvy form when he finished tied for twenty-third in the Tour Championship in Georgia. He carded rounds of 71, 68, 72 and 76 to end up with a 7-over-par 287. That may have sounded like failure, given that the winner, Brandt Snedeker, finished with a 10-under-par 270, but Rickie – who was a 100–1 shot to win the event – did finish ahead of the likes of Lee Westwood and Ernie Els. The course was no walkover and it was old-timer Tiger Woods who made the early running with a four-under-par sixty-six on Thursday to share the first-round lead with Justin Rose. Jim Furyk then took over the leader's mantle after a second round with a one-stroke advantage. As the fourth round began on the Sunday, Snedeker and Justin Rose were tied for the lead, with the American proving the eventual victor.

Snedeker's win also meant he ended top in the FedExCup standings and pocketed $10 million for his achievement.

Rickie had also finished in the top thirty – no mean feat in just his third season as a pro golfer – landing at number twenty-eight in the standings and taking home $185,000 for his efforts.

Rickie was then hit with another problem as he prepared to compete in a couple of tournaments as September merged into October in 2012. Now, he had to contend with a back injury too and was forced to withdraw. He explained in a short statement, 'I am sorry to confirm, but I will not be competing in the KOLON Korea Open next week, nor the CIMB Classic the following week in Malaysia as planned. Unfortunately, while not serious, I have battled a back issue for the past few months, and my doctors have instructed me that international travel and any tournament play is not in my best interest at this time.' It was rotten luck, as he had been looking forward to defending his Korea Open crown.

It was two months before he finally felt able to return to the golf course in a pro tournament, when he turned up at Thousand Oaks in California for the World Challenge presented by Northwestern Mutual. Considering he had been laid up for such a stretch, he did remarkably well, finishing tied for fourth with Tiger Woods and Jim Furyk. Graeme McDowell topped the final leader board and exited with a cheque for $1 million. But Rickie was happy with his own performance and the $200,000 he pocketed for a more than satisfactory weekend's work. Rickie carded rounds of 73, 67, 70 and 69 for a 9-under-par total of 279. Afterwards, he admitted at a press conference he was simply glad to be back in business after his layoff. He said, 'All in all it was a great week, nice to come back after a few months off. The game feels good and it was nice to get out and back in competition. Not exactly in contention where I want to be, but a good week overall – and a fun week too.'

And how was the old back faring? Any twinges? 'The back feels good,' he said. 'I've still got a little way to go with it but it's been a good week to test it. I'll be playing at the Shark Shootout next week and I'm looking forward to continuing to get better. My game feels like it's in a good place and I'm looking forward to the 2013 season.'

He completed 2012 with that appointment at the 'Shark' the following week. The event – officially named the Franklin Templeton Shootout in 2012 – is famed for helping youth charities and Rickie, who has always made a point of supporting charity work, was delighted to take part. It was a chance to further ease himself back into the scheme of things while also benefitting good causes. And he had always loved playing as a team with other pros – in this event, he would be part of a two-man outfit along with his pal Bud Cauley. The tournament in Naples, Florida was, as ever, hosted by Greg Norman, from whom the moniker 'the Shark Shootout' originated, as Greg was widely known as 'The Great White Shark' in his 1980s heyday. Defending champions Keegan Bradley and Brendan Steele were aiming to secure back-to-back titles.

But it was Rickie and Bud who would earn a pat on

the back from Nicklaus after their impressive first round saw them card sixty-six. Norman invited the pair to join him at the driving range for a family golf clinic. 'We have Rickie Fowler and Bud Cauley, two of the best swingers on the PGA Tour today,' Norman said by way of introduction to the crowd, who lapped up the tips and exhibition shots from them. But it was Kenny Perry and Sean O'Hair who won the tournament with a final score of 185 after the 3 rounds played – a massive 31-under-par. Rickie and Bud ended up in ninth place after a 20-under-par total of 196. Both were pleased with their efforts and Rickie was particularly bubbly afterwards – he was getting back into his old routine and his back hadn't played him up over the three days.

It was a good end to a year that had been wonderful in patches, generally on the up from the previous season but with a worryingly disappointing series of results in the middle section.

Rickie headed off to Hawaii for the holiday season with family and friends and the sole intention of letting his hair down by mountain biking, swimming in the sea and surfing. It was a chance to get away from it all and it was just what he needed to recharge his batteries before hitting the tour circuit again in January 2013. He came back refreshed and ready to go. The boy was always moving forward: he hated treading water and was determined to improve once again. That had become the yardstick by which he was now happy to determine his fortunes. If he could go one better each year, he would be a happy man. Rickie Fowler was on his way to the very top of the golfing world – his commitment and attitude left no doubt about that.

CHAPTER ELEVEN

LUCKY THIRTEEN

At the very start of 2013 Rickie was doing what he always loved to do as the festive season merged into the new year – having fun. It is a word that is synonymous with the man – the word he uses most both when at play and when playing golf. He is a young man who loves life and likes to live it to the full; he works hard and plays hard. But he never plays hard in a self-destructive way – booze, drugs and lots of women have never been for Rickie. He loves to relax by indulging in his outdoor passions – mountain biking, swimming, diving and surfing – and enjoys good food with his family and friends. So those were the factors that helped him decide to spend the start of 2013 in one of his favourite places on the planet: Hawaii.

Another factor that influenced his decision was that he would also be able to truly mix business with pleasure, as the season opener would take place on the beautiful Hawaiian island of Maui and, more specifically, at the Kapalua golf resort. Maui is the second largest of the Hawaiian islands at 727 square miles and its beauty has long resonated with Rickie. Even the PGA were caught rhapsodising about the island that would play host to the winners of the previous year's tournaments, saying, 'Few courses in the world feature as many breathtaking views as the Plantation Course at Kapalua in Maui. This week, the Tour is in paradise for the 2011 winners-only Hyundai Tournament of Champions. There's been a little tweak this year in order to accommodate fans. Rather than the traditional Thursday start, the Tournament of Champions will begin on Friday and have a Monday finish. That means it won't have to compete with the NFL playoffs with a Sunday finish.'

Rickie arrived at Kapalua looking healthy and sounding confident, although he did admit that he had suffered with his back problem and that it had affected him for much longer than he had initially admitted. So the decision to turn the event into a three, rather than four-day contest may have suited Rickie as he worked his way back to fitness and form. In public, he had only really touched upon his back condition as being an unwelcome distraction at the latter end of 2012 but now he conceded that it had actually been playing up and causing him problems since the early summer of that year; that he had felt the pain but tried to keep it hidden away, as he didn't want it to be seen as an excuse if he failed to deliver in the big tournaments.

Speaking in Maui before the PGA Tour's season-opening Hyundai Tournament of Champions, Rickie told how the pain in his lower back affected him from the time of the US Open in June and that he was advised by medics that his lower back and hips were inflamed and that he needed to go easy. He tried to take their advice, taking a month off before the Open Championship in Britain but, even then, he remained uncomfortable with the twinges. 'It was not fun with how I felt,' he admitted, although he played on with the aid of painkillers.

The diagnosis of how he had come to have the problem in the first place stressed to him that he would need to adapt his stance when playing if he were to overcome the condition, explaining, 'If you look at your posture when you set up and when I was getting into my backswing – two years ago, my back bend went forward at the top of my backswing and I was actually going the other way. It was only a difference in like five degrees, but it was more that it had gone from either staying in posture or forward to kind of bending backwards, which doesn't really work well in the low back.'

Rickie told how he had dealt with the problem by adjusting his stance when he played, so that he would not increase the pressure on his lower back. 'If you don't work on your alignment on a day-to-day basis or week-to-week basis, your eyes start to go one way and you start to compensate, and two weeks, three weeks down the road, you've aimed left but it feels like you've aimed right,' said Fowler. 'So it's just the little things, but we'll definitely be on top of check-ups going forward.'

It was, perhaps, telling that, directly before the problem flared up, he had notched up four top-ten finishes while, after its onset, he hit that middle section of the year when many things did not fall into place as he would have hoped. The disappointing results could probably now be seen in their true light – that he had been struggling with lower-back pain and could no longer play his normal game. So he struggled to put together a run of good results as he tried to adapt to his new situation. Now, in Maui, Rickie admitted that, indeed, that had been the case:

I had some really good finishes and got my first win, which was awesome. Then it may have looked kind of funny after that but I was keeping a secret for a while as I played on while injured. I was trying to do my best to get through. I wanted to make it through the Tour Championship, which I did. Then I was working toward the Ryder Cup, but I fell a little short there.

But I took some time off for rehab of my lower back and definitely now feel that I am heading in the right direction. I'm still not one hundred per cent but feel my swing is better and that I am playing well. It just feels good to be back in competition. And after the two-month break I had, it fuelled the fire a little bit to come back. It made me want to play and compete more.

Rickie said he was particularly pleased to be in Maui with some of his good golfing pals:

It's actually my second trip here. I don't remember my first one. I think I was like three or something. So it's my first real trip to Maui. I've been hanging out with a couple of my Red Bull buddies – Ian Walsh and Kyle Lenny live just outside Peahi and I've hung out there a little bit.

I'm planning to go back over there next week when the tournament is finished and I'm just enjoying some time on the island, getting used to the life over here. Today was my third round of golf since I've been here – I've been balancing fun and golf at the same time and have been enjoying it. But I'm looking forward to getting things started tomorrow.

And what hopes and dreams did he have for 2013? 'I definitely want to make sure I'm ready to play every time that I tee it up,' he said. 'I want to be in contention more often and work towards having a multiple-win season. I finally got the first one out of the way last year, so I'll be trying to pick off a few more. I want to free my mind up so that I keep playing well. Off the course, I want to grow my brand and my fan base and work with charity.'

A swift analysis of his work and results during 2012 and 2013 proves instructive. On paper, you could contend that the former was the more successful year in that he won one PGA tournament, while in 2013 he would not win any. But dig a little deeper and it could be argued that 2013 was more successful in terms of overall progress, in that Rickie achieved five top-ten finishes in both years but did so over less tournaments in 2013 than in 2012. In 2012 the five finishes were gained in twenty-three tournaments but a year later he managed it in twenty-two. But 2012 was definitely better for his bank balance – that year he banked a total of $3,066,293 but a year later considerably less, with a grand total of $1,816,742. In 2012 he finished twenty-first on the money list but he only finished fortieth a year later.

Yet 2013 saw him end up with a slightly better average round figure – 70.21 as opposed to 70.61 in the previous year. His main disappointment would be that he would not win a tournament in 2013 and that his best finish was a tied for third. However, this was the year when his main rivals – especially Rory McIlroy – hit their best form and dominated proceedings, so Rickie never let it get him down. He was positive enough in his own ability and intelligent enough to know that, like most things in sporting life, golf successes and domination tended to move in cycles. He steadfastly felt that his cycle – and his era of dominance – would come if he kept on working hard, improving and believing in himself and his ever-developing talent.

And Rickie certainly made a steady start to achieving his work aims as he finished a credible tied for sixth place at the Hyundai in Maui with three-round cards of 70, 74 and 67 – an 8-under-par total of 211. He declared himself 'happy' with his performance and the outcome, saying it was a satisfactory start to his year and one that gave him confidence and that he could build on for the busy, demanding season that lay ahead.

Three weeks later he again finished tied for sixth, this time at the Farmers Insurance Open at La Jolla in California. That earned him $204,350 and, once again, he nodded his head and smiled as he told the press corps that it had been a good result. Before the event, the pundits at *PGA.com* had highlighted their top-ten tips for who might win. Phil Mickelson and Tiger Woods headed the field and Rickie, funnily enough, was viewed as the sixth most likely to triumph. They stated, 'Farmers University Day is Saturday, preceding Fowler's traditional Sunday OSU attire. That's a lot of orange in 48 hours, to go along with his usual red numbers at Torrey, where Rickie has never finished out of the top 20.'

As well as his sixth-place finish, Rickie had also been cheered up by getting involved in some free-time – and giving his time for free – voluntary work before the tournament officially got underway. As we have mentioned, he is very much a young man who believes in putting something back into the game that has given him so much. He loves helping youngsters and seeing their faces light up when he turns up to meet them. A few days before the Farmers teed off, he headed for San Diego to host a youth golf clinic in conjunction with Farmers Insurance at the Century Club. The event saw Rickie and fellow golfer and pal Charley Hoffman put on an hour-long golf demonstration for kids of all ages at Mission Bay Golf Club, which each year donates to nearly a hundred youth and educational organisations. The first 500 youngsters to arrive also each received a special commemorative gift from the star duo.

The Farmers Insurance group spoke of their appreciation that Rickie and Charley had put themselves out for no fee to help bring some joy to the area's youngsters – and, hopefully, potential golfing geniuses of the future! 'Having these two PGA Tour stars share their knowledge and experience about being winners – both on and off the golf course – will leave a lasting impression on the young people participating in today's event,' said Mhayse Samalya, an executive with Farmers Insurance. 'Also, as a precursor to the upcoming Farmers Insurance Open, this youth golf clinic provides a clear demonstration of our commitment to giving back to the communities we are proud to serve.'

The group also paid its respects to Rickie and what he had already achieved in his brief professional career, saying, 'Rickie Fowler grew up playing golf in Southern California and is almost entirely self-taught. Fowler starred at Murrieta Valley High School before playing college golf at Oklahoma State. He joined the PGA Tour in 2010 where he earned Rookie of the Year honours. Fowler is now one of the hottest players on the Tour after his head-to-head victory over Rory McIlroy at the Wells Fargo Championship.'

It became clear just why Rickie particularly enjoys playing at the Farmers Insurance Open every year, as the event garners millions of dollars for young people – something he loves to be a part of. The publicists for the Farmers group explained, 'The 2012 Farmers Insurance Open generated more than $2 million to deserving organisations, several of which were in attendance at last year's clinic. These organisations included Pro Kids Golf Academy and Learning Centre, The San Diego Junior Golf Association and Boys and Girls Clubs.'

On the golf course itself, the Farmers Insurance of 2013 was also notable for the return to form of Tiger Woods, who won the tournament and, with it, a cheque for $1,098,000. Woods triumphed with a 14-under-par total of 274, compared to Rickie's 8-under-par 280. It was the seventh time he had won the event – a tournament that has seen him as victor more than any tournament during his long career. It was also his seventy-career win – a statistic you cannot argue with.

For Rickie, solid progress with committed, honest endeavours would always be behind his own progress to the top of the trade. It was telling that, during the week of the tournament, it was also announced that he had tied up a deal with the Farmers Insurance group to become an ambassador for them. He would wear their logo on his golfing hats but the link-up was about much more than another sponsorship deal. He believed in the altruistic nature of the group and what they had done and planned to do to help young people. Their aims ran parallel to his own and those of his Rickie Fowler Foundation to help children in sport and education, so it was a natural move that they should work together.

'We are very excited about partnering with Rickie and having him as an ambassador for the Farmers brand and for the charities and educational initiatives we support through golf and our other sponsorships,' said Mike Linton, Enterprise Chief Marketing Officer for Farmers Insurance. 'Farmers Insurance and Rickie Fowler have shared common interests when it comes to the importance of education.'

Rickie was equally pleased with the link-up, saying, 'I am looking forward to teaming up with Farmers Insurance because we have a lot in common. What really stands out is the way Farmers Insurance is committed to the communities it serves and does business in and its focus on educational, charitable and civic programs such as First Tee.'

Rickie was in a great mood as he headed from California to the next venue in the following week on the PGA tour. As he arrived in Scottsdale, Arizona, for the Waste Management Phoenix Open, he was determined to improve on his previous season's tied for twenty-sixth finish but it didn't turn out as he wished. Instead, he was left reflecting on his first case of missing a cut in 2013, much to his disappointment. Both he and playing partner Jason Dufner finished the second round on 3-under-par 139s, so Dufner joined Rickie in packing his bags early.

Rickie fared much better at the Honda Classic at the end of February and beginning of March 2013. He made the cut this time and ended up tied for thirteenth, with a 1-under-par 4-round total of 279. The competitors all had to deal with a troublesome side wind, which knocked some off course, but Rickie claimed to enjoy working in the conditions. At the end of a fine third-round of sixty-nine, he said of the conditions, 'I just love using my imagination, coming up with different shots and trying to use the wind as my friend. It tricks up the golf course a little bit and makes you play a little differently.'

And would he go for the same approach on the final day – trying to use the wind to his benefit, rather than focusing on it negatively? 'Well, I haven't looked at the forecast but I know it's supposed to be pretty similar. So, yes, I will go for the same game plan. I'll come out for a little practice in the morning, get some food, warm up and head to the tee. I've been hitting a lot of good putts and I've just got to try to keep the ball in the short grass.'

Unfortunately, he only carded a seventy-four on the final day and that left him outside the top ten where he had reckoned on finishing.

Next up were two tournaments that he and the other pros used as preparation for the first Major of the season: the Masters at Augusta. First up was the Cadillac Championship, followed by the Arnold Palmer Invitational. In 2011 Rickie had finished in eighth place at the Cadillac – a fine result, given that he was still in only his second full season as a pro – and tied for thirtieth in the Arnold Palmer. Similar results in 2013 provided a real boost for Fowler as he continued his own preparations for the Masters. He had always made it plain that winning a Major was one of his big dreams and to slip on the green jacket as the winner of the Masters was the biggest dream for most golfers, given its legendary status, wonderful greens and iconic history.

Rickie found the going difficult at the Cadillac but gave himself a real boost at the Arnold Palmer – his final event before heading out to Augusta. A tied-for-thirty-fifth finish at the Cadillac was a real disappointment but a tied-for-third conclusion at the Arnold Palmer gave him real hope that he could make an impact at the Masters. Tiger Woods was also thinking exactly the same after he beat Rickie to win the event – his third win of a season that appeared to signify great hope for the former Golden Boy of golf.

Woods won with a 4-round, 13-under par total of 275, with Justin Rose two strokes behind as runner-up. Rickie, Keegan Bradley and Gonzalo Fernandez-Casta all tied for third with 8-under-par 280s – and each with a cheque for approaching $300,000 apiece. Woods's finish meant he usurped McIlroy at the top of the rankings – the first time in eight months that Rory had not been top of the pile. And it was Rickie who had been the main challenger to Tiger as they approached the final three holes. Unfortunately, Rickie struggled on the sixteenth, hitting his second shot into the water, while playing partner Tiger surged onwards and upwards.

At the post-event press conference, Rickie was asked if it had been intimidating taking on Woods one-to-one – had it maybe even affected his confidence and subsequent performance? No, he replied, mistakes can happen to anyone at any time. It wasn't the first time he had worked the greens with the new world number one and, no doubt, it wouldn't be the last. Commenting on his own round, Rickie admitted,

'Up until sixteen, I felt really good. I was swinging it well, I made a few putts and tried to put a little pressure on the others. It was just unfortunate to make that swing at that time. If I'd had a good shot then, it would have put a little pressure on him [Woods] coming into the last two holes.' During the tournament, he felt he had done well, even on the final round, apart from the mess-up on the sixteenth, 'I felt really comfortable out there. I stayed patient, made a lot of pars and finally made a birdie on nine. I felt I settled into the round and that was the best I felt in the final group.'

Rickie was on course for the Masters – he was feeling confident in himself and confident in his golf. Of course, there were a few errors that had crept in, such as the sixteenth water shot at the Arnold Palmer, but Rickie accepted that as part of the process of streamlining his game as the season progressed. And a third-place finish at the Arnold Palmer suggested he was making more good decisions than blunders in his quest for a second PGA win and that elusive first Major triumph.

The week before the Masters, he committed to taking part in the Tavistock Cup. This was a tournament in which he could truly have fun and help others less fortunate than himself. It is a two-day team event played in Florida, which features the top-ranked pros from six golf clubs: Albany, Isleworth, Lake Nona, Oak Tree National, Primland, and Queenwood. Four pros from each club play for prize money, hole-in-one prizes and to help charities and worthwhile causes. Player charities and youth and community groups are the chief beneficiaries and millions of dollars have gone to such worthy organisations.

Given the nature of the event and the fact that it was a chance to relax and have fun, it seemed a no-brainer for Rickie to take part. It was another step in his build-up to the Masters but he was able to go about his business with a more relaxed attitude and know he was helping charity at the same time. Rickie played for Team Oak Tree National along with his pals Scott Verplank, Bob Tway and Charlie Howell. As an indication of the strength of the competition, Team Albany included Tiger Woods, Justin Rose and Ian Poulter!

It was, therefore, hardly surprising that Albany – with fourth member Tim Clark supplementing the 'big beasts' – ended up triumphant out of the six teams. Rickie and his cohorts finished fifth but he admitted after the tournament that winning was not just what it was about for him; he enjoyed the friendly atmosphere and the fact that the stress levels were not as high as for an individual PGA event. Although the tournament is officially sanctioned by the PGA, it does not count towards rankings or points. There were cash incentives for the teams, although they were not sanctioned by the PGA. The winning team received $600,000 to split between them, the runners-up $400,000, the third placed got $300,000 and each player on the fourth, fifth and sixth teams took home $50,000 apiece.

So Rickie walked away with a nice cheque in his pocket, but it was never about the money for him. 'He knows exactly how fortunate he is to have such an enviable lifestyle – doing something he loves as a job and being with people he likes,' a US PGA spokesman said. They went on to say:

> And the great thing with Rickie is that he is one of the most generous, kindest, caring and thoughtful guys in the PGA. He's not a guy who holds grudges or is spiteful; if he loses he just shrugs his shoulders and looks to the next challenge. Not that he is not committed or determined to win the biggest prizes – because he is definitely a man who wants to be the best – but he believes in respecting his opponents and doing things the right way. He is a dedicated Christian and a really nice guy too, who is well liked by everyone on the Tour.

The PGA summed up the final outcome and what it meant in an official statement after the event, saying:

> The event, shortened to one day of stroke play because of the Monday finish to the Arnold Palmer Invitational presented by MasterCard, saw four-man teams from Albany and Lake Nona finish the day at 7-over, tied for the lowest composite total in the six-team field. Poulter, who shot a team-low 72 Tuesday at Isleworth, was joined by Tiger Woods (73), Tim Clark (73) and Justin Rose (77) on the victorious side. Woods joined Poulter in the best-ball play-off against Lake Nona's Graeme McDowell and Henrik Stenson. McDowell carded a 71 to be one of just two players in red numbers for the

day. Ross Fisher (72), Stenson (74) and Peter Hanson (78) rounded out the scoring for Lake Nona. Primland and host team Isleworth finished one shot off the pace while Oak Tree National was 12-over and Queenwood was 20-over. Webb Simpson, representing Primland, had the day's best round: a 2-under 70.

No mention of Rickie, although there was confirmation that he and his teammates had finished fifth with a twelve-over total. No matter – as he said himself later, it was the workout and the enjoyment that counted most for him. He had prepared well and was in high spirits as he exited the Tavistock Cup and headed home for a few days. Now he would rest and practise until he felt even more confident that he was ready: a date with Augusta and the Masters loomed ever closer.

CHAPTER TWELVE

YOU GOTTA HAVE FAITH

The Masters is THE Major as far as American golfers are concerned. Sure, it meant a lot to win the US PGA, the British Open and the US Open: they were prestigious tournaments and conferred glory and honour upon their winners. But the Masters was something altogether more legendary, mythical and even mystical. To win at Augusta elevated the golfer to a different level and meant his name would forever live on in the annals of the sport's pantheon. Indeed, this event bestowed legendary status on those gifted enough to wear its famous green jacket. So it was little surprise that Rickie Fowler wanted to make an impact on the tournament. Like his fellow Americans, he approached the event with an extra knot of anxiety and expectation – who wouldn't if success would propel them towards golfing immortality? Rickie's dream was to win the Masters in front of his own fans and to celebrate victory with them. It was the all-American dream – the dream of all American golfers and golf fans, that is – to achieve or to witness a big piece of sporting history unfolding; to be able to win it as a golfer and to have been there to see the win as a fan.

A win at Augusta for Rickie would propel his career into orbit. His fan base would increase, his sponsorship deals would be all the more valuable and he would be able to negotiate new contracts. But for all that, there would be something more important for Rickie – the joy it would bring him, his family and his ever-growing army of fans. As he said, he had enough money to retire now if he wanted and enough deals to keep the readies coming in for years. But Rickie had always been about more than materialistic rewards: for him, doing his best and being the best – but at the same time always being an honourable, decent guy – was what mattered most. This was a young man with principles and a clear knowledge of right and wrong.

It was a result of his solid upbringing and his determination to live his life by the boundaries of the Christian faith he was committed to. So as he approached the Augusta National course in April 2013, he took a deep breath at the full scale of its beauty – and potential to launch him to superstardom. It was the first Major of 2013 and Rickie made a point of enjoying himself and the wonderful greens before the action teed off. The Wednesday before, he embarked upon a practice round – and had his grandmother be his caddy!

Rickie also decided to entertain his fans with some daring

shots as he and his gran made their way around the course. On the sixteenth hole, he had no hesitation in sending a shot across the water and on to the green, much to the delight of the fans that followed him. And, given the difficulty of the shot, he did well to land it not far from the hole. As an exercise in gelling with his fans, it was a real success but it also showed he was in a relaxed but confident mood as the Thursday teeing-off moved ever closer.

Later on the Wednesday, he even joked about taking his grandmother on the practice round, saying he had taken his granddad as his caddy the first year he had played the Masters and his father in the second year, so now it was the turn of his grandmother to accompany him. When asked how she had been as a caddy, he said, 'She did great. I think she's actually supposed to have knee surgery at some point coming up but, all of a sudden, her knee felt pretty good today. She kept me calm. She was good. She did a good job on the back [nine] and we had fun. A Wednesday afternoon [with his grandmother] around Augusta is pretty special.'

He also explained once again that his grandfather had a special place in his heart as it was he who encouraged Rickie to take up the game, and that his gran was not a bad golfer either. He had played rounds with both of them in the past.

But a day later, it was a much more focused and serious Rickie who teed off as the tournament got underway. You could see just what the event meant to him and how professionally he was taking it as he stormed to a fine opening round of sixty-eight. That put him toward the top of the leader board, tied for fourth at four-under-par. Above him were Marc Leishman and Sergio Garcia, both on six-under-par after rounds of sixty-six, and Dustin Johnson, who was a point behind the leading pair and a stroke ahead of Rickie.

Yet despite Rickie's impressive start, certain members of the press were more inclined to criticise him for his colourful dress sense. The *Bleacher Report* said:

> Fowler emerged from the clubhouse wearing a lime green outfit that may have ruined high-definition television as we know it … it's wholly fair to say Fowler's outfit stole the spotlight – if only because it's possible that the outfit itself had a spotlight attached … it's both bemusing and comforting to see that Fowler refuses to change due to his surroundings. The Masters is a tradition unlike any other, but its rules and regulations have the personality of a public library. Conservative, proper dress is required – a fact that, while within Augusta National's rules, Fowler thumbs his nose at here.

But no one could deny that his opening statement of sixty-eight had been impressive. It was the best round of all the younger stars at Augusta and even earned a place in the history books, according to *ESPN*, who tweeted: 'Rickie Fowler is 1st golfer with 2 double-bogeys in round at The Masters to shoot in the 60s since Raymond Floyd in 1992.' Rickie said his improved form had been as a result of his back pain decreasing and that he no longer had to worry about it flaring up as he walked around the greens. He told the press:

> My back is definitely starting to feel a lot better. Bay Hill [the Arnold Palmer Invitational a couple of weeks before the Masters] was the first 72-hole event I was able to play without any medication. So I'm definitely on the upswing on the health side of things with my back. It's nice to not have to worry about it as much.
>
> The swing is feeling good. I made a couple of swirly swings today, but it's nice to play with less pain than last year. That was not a fun eight months from June onwards but now I am excited about where my game is and I definitely feel more comfortable and confident.

Rickie admitted that he enjoyed seeing his name at the top of the leader board as he went about carding that fine sixty-eight. He said, 'It was funny seeing them put my name and scores up on the leader board when I was on 16 green. I thought, "Oh, this is going to be interesting," seeing all the numbers. I had a look around and noticed that Marc was playing well today. It's great just being here for the Masters and getting to play Augusta. But now I've got to focus on my game and get into good position going into Sunday.'

His ambition was admirable but he wasn't able to keep up the good work during the next three days. He struggled on his second round, carding a disappointing seventy-six after suffering a triple-bogey on that testing sixteenth hole. He did better on his third round, slicing six strokes off that seventy-six from the previous day to end with a seventy. He said he was pleased to have improved his play on the Saturday and that he was happy with the seventy, as he had initially found it hard to get going. 'I got off to a bit of a slow start but made a nice eagle on eight. That jump-started things and I then played a little bit better than yesterday. I hit a lot more greens and that made it a little less stressful. I've got a few things to straighten out on the [practice] range and then I'll see if I can make a run tomorrow.'

He was extra pleased with his day, as the conditions had been more testing than on the previous one. He said, 'It played a little tougher today – the greens are a bit firmer. So I'm definitely happy with where I ended up.' Certainly, he was of the opinion that his game was getting better all the time. Rickie explained:

> This is my third year here and I now feel comfortable. I've played enough rounds to know my way around and I just feel I'm getting more comfortable going into each Major.

Unfortunately, he wasn't able to translate that 'feel-good factor' into his game on the final day of the Masters. Rickie finished with a round of 78, which meant he ended up with a 4-over-par total of 292 and was tied for thirty-eighth. In the previous year he had finished tied for twenty-seventh with a total of 290 and in 2011 he finished tied for thirty-eighth with a total of 291. So, on paper at least, he had not progressed with his form at the Masters over those three years. But, looking at it more reasonably, the truth of it was that Rickie had been treading water – he was placed more or less in the same positions and his totals were not that different in the three-year spell.

You could argue that it was positive proof that he was not making as much solid progress as he had hoped for but he believed he was moving forward and that, now he had finally beaten his back pain, he would set new markers for himself. It is often difficult – and dangerous and unfair – to set down three lots of statistics from three different years, as the stark figures do not necessarily reflect the conditions the golfer faced in each year and the competition from ever-improving rivals the golfer had also to contend with. Certainly, Rickie did not feel downhearted about his results from the 2013 Masters. He felt he was still improving and had enough humility to accept that he was also still learning. He was young and each experience benefitted him, turning him into a world-class golfer at the end of the process.

Every tournament and every year provided him with the tools he needed to be in a position to challenge Rory McIlroy and the other stars of the circuit. Rickie had watched his Australian rival Adam Scott slip on the legendary green jacket as the Masters wrapped up for another year and had drawn inspiration from his success. He was eight years older than Rickie and had moved up through the ranks, learning after each tournament, to win at Augusta. It was his first Major triumph and would be followed by a spell as world number one. It was a peak that had been reached through hard work,

100 per cent commitment and endeavour. All his successes and disappointments before that Masters joy had moulded him into the golfer he had become. He had even had to battle the odds to win at Augusta, emerging from the chasing pack on the final day to threaten the leaders and, ultimately, had to also survive a tense, sudden-death play-off to see off the equally determined and revved-up Angel Cabrera in order to lift the title. It meant that Scott had become the first Australian to win the Masters – at 32 years old. Rickie still had time on his side and he was patient enough, focused enough and measured enough to know that, if he kept on doing what he was doing, he would also reach the promised land of lifting a Major when the time was right and he was ready.

Like Rickie, Scott was humbled when he tasted success, as his acceptance speech conveyed. After his victory, Scott said, 'It fell my way today. There was some luck there but it's incredible to be in this position. I'm honoured. This is the one thing in golf we hadn't been able to achieve. It's amazing that it's my destiny to be the first Australian to win.' Scott also showed that, again like Rickie, he was not so self-obsessed that he couldn't see how others had helped and inspired him. He dedicated the win to fellow Australian and golfing legend Greg Norman, saying, 'There was one guy who inspired a nation of golfers and that's Greg Norman. He's been incredible to me and part of this definitely belongs to him. A phone conversation's not going to do it; we're very close. I would love to share a beer with him and talk through it all. To anyone near my age, Greg was the best player in the world: an icon.'

Rickie left Augusta with the thought that he could also do an Adam Scott and win the Masters. He was confident enough in his own ability to believe that it would one day be the case and he would battle on until the big breakthrough finally came. But he was also wise enough to accept that his problem right now – and, indeed, since he had turned pro – was a lack of consistency. He would go a handful of tournaments finishing well up the leader board but would then struggle to maintain that excellence in the next batch of events. It had been the story of his life so far as a pro: somehow, he needed to ensure he finished well in every event. He would work hard on trying to bring about that elusive consistency over the next twelve months but it would not be easy.

His final placing at the Masters had been disappointing after that wonderful first-round sixty-eight and, as usual, he then followed that up with five further let-downs. Then his good form would return and he would do well in the four events that followed the five disappointments. It was enough to make Rickie tear his hair out but, of course, he was not that type of character. Instead, he accepted that there was a problem and worked his darndest to overcome the setbacks.

After the Masters, he headed off to New Orleans for the Zurich Classic. The organisers and local press in Louisiana were delighted that Rickie would be appearing – it showed how he was viewed as one of the rising stars of the PGA and how his attendance would bring the crowds flocking in. The boy was box-office material. The local New Orleans paper,

The Times-Picayune, heralded his imminent arrival with some pomp, pointing out that:

> At least one of the Golf Boys will be in New Orleans this year. Rising star Rickie Fowler, who won his first PGA Tour event one week after last year's Zurich Classic, has committed to play in the 2013 tournament here. Fowler, 24, captured the Wells Fargo Championship in Charlotte last year a week after tying for 10th place in New Orleans. The next week, he finished tied for second place at The Players Championship at Ponte Vedra Beach. Fowler, known for his golf wardrobe and bright orange on Sundays to honor his alma mater, Oklahoma State, is part of the Golf Boys group, which consists of himself, Bubba Watson, Ben Crane and Hunter Mahan. They recently released another video titled, Golf Boys 2. Oh.

Steve Worthy, CEO of the Fore! Kids Foundation, which organises the Zurich Classic, was also keen to trumpet Rickie's CV to the media. He said, 'Rickie Fowler has already established himself as one of the brightest young players on the PGA Tour, and his top 10 finish here at the Zurich Classic last year teed him up for his first career victory the very next week.'

The trumpeting of Rickie's talent and star appeal by the locals did make one very pertinent point – he could use the tournament as a springboard for another assault on the

Wells Fargo, where he was the holder. And many pundits believed that Rickie could not only use the event to prepare for the Wells Fargo but that he could actually win the Zurich Classic. The *sportsunbiased.com* team led with a headline proclaiming: ZURICH CLASSIC PREVIEW/PREDICTION: RICKIE FOWLER VICTORIOUS. The piece then explained just why they had backed Rickie: 'He made the cut in seven of his eight starts this season. Of the seven cuts he made he managed to record four top-25s, three top-10s and a third place finish. He managed a tie for 10th in last year's edition of this event. Fowler is 24th in driving accuracy, ninth in sand save percentage, 15th in the all-around and 13th on tour in total putting. Rickie is chomping at the bit to taste victory again. This might be the week.'

And the bloggers behind the excellent *downthe18th* site in the Midlands, England, also reckoned Rickie would triumph in New Orleans and confirmed the widely held surprise that such a talented golfer had not won more than just the Wells Fargo tournament. Pointing out that Rickie was also rated at odds of 22–1 with bookmakers Coral, they added:

We can't believe that Rickie only has 1 PGA title to his name so far, and yet he is regarded as one of the best in the game. So it's definitely about time he picked up his 2nd. We have been watching quite a bit of Rickie of late, and he's ready this week for sure. He is currently 22nd in strokes gained-putting, 16th scrambling, 15th all-round, 46th total driving and 9th sand saves for those

71 bunkers out there. His form is respectable all round, 38th at Augusta and then 3rd, 35th and 13th the weeks before that. Around here he has gone 26th and then 10th in 2012. Other than his last PGA Championship performance, Rickie fits the bill this week.

But despite all the encouragement, Rickie could not find his best form in New Orleans. Much like the Masters, he started off at speed with a solid sixty-six but lost impetus with rounds of seventy-three and seventy-one. The big difference here was that he did manage to put in a good final round – a rousing sixty-eight. But his total of 279 – 9-under-par – meant he finished among the also-rans. He was tied for thirty-second.

It hadn't gone to plan but worse was to come when Rickie returned to the scene of his greatest triumph. Only a year earlier he had won the Wells Fargo at Quail Hollow in Charlotte but now he would have the letters MDF alongside his name, meaning: Made the cut but Did not Finish. On the final leader board, he was ranked tied for seventy-third. It was a wretched comedown for the man who had been welcomed and feted only a few days earlier as the course champion. He carded two rounds of seventy-two and a seventy-seven and failed to even make the fourth round after that poor third-round finish on seventy-seven. He had fallen foul of the MDF rule, which is akin to a second cut for those golfers who could not even make the top seventy. From the previous year's rise to glory, Rickie's fall from grace had been just as emphatic – and chastening rather than joyful.

Yet it had all started so well when he turned up for his first press conference as reigning champion. He said he was glad to be back and that the return had brought back pleasant memories, adding: 'Yeah, it's fun to be back. It's the first time I've been here since I won last year, so I'm just reliving memories this week and enjoying being back. I'm also enjoying seeing a lot of the staff and tournament committee and some of the players from last year. I feel like I'm the big man on campus right now, so it's kind of cool. I'm looking forward to playing [practising] today and getting ready to play the tournament tomorrow.'

That phrase 'the big man on campus' would come back to haunt Rickie as he blew his chance to retain his title. But it was only a saying; his feet were still on the ground, as he made clear when he was asked if his win had led to his fellow pros treating him any differently. He joked and said he was still treated 'as a little kid' by his older rivals. Rickie admitted, 'Things haven't changed a whole lot. I guess now that I'm [on] a PGA Tour, there is a little more credibility but, other than that, I don't get treated any differently … Maybe after I win ten, fifteen, twenty events, then they might look at me a little differently but we'll work on the second one for now.'

He also conceded that it had been good to 'get the monkey off my back' by winning that first PGA tournament but added that it did, however, also make expectations for further immediate success to increase. 'It was nice to get the monkey off the back for sure,' he said, going on:

For my own sake and to stop the questions about it – whether it was from the media or the fans. But I felt like I had higher expectations for myself, so I wasn't really worried about what anyone else thought. But it was definitely nice to get the first one out of the way and move forward.

This next year I want to work on winning multiple times and playing well in the FedEx Cup. The goals are within reach and show I have high expectations of myself. I know I belong out here and I know I can win out here. I don't ever want to show up at a week of a tournament and not think I'm playing to win. I want to be in contention every week and I want to be fighting for a trophy. I've been playing well this year, working on some swing stuff and getting my back healthy and I feel like I'm heading in the right direction.

He added that he was generally pleased with his performances and that he believed he would achieve more glory in 2013. Rickie said:

I've had a couple of solid finishes. I've only been in the mix a couple of times, most recently at Bay Hill. I had to take a chance at Tiger on the sixteenth hole but, unfortunately, got one a little heavy. But I felt good letting him know that I was around, making a couple of putts and that I wasn't going to back down. So I'm looking forward to getting back in that position and, hopefully, that will be this week as it was last year. I feel like I'm heading in the right direction with my swing, with what I'm doing with my trainer in the gym and my soft-tissue guys and by making sure that my body's healthy and working properly. I'm excited moving forward and looking forward to playing through the summer healthy, unlike last year.

Rickie would not be so optimistic in his beliefs when he became a big-name victim of the MDF rule due to him finishing outside the top seventy. By any standards, it was a gut-wrenching fall from grace and, in my opinion, it took him a good month to get over the disappointment. In the next three tournaments in May 2013, he would end the final rounds with finishes of missing the cut, tied for fifty-fourth and tied for thirty-seventh. It was only after the latter of those setbacks that he finally returned to something approaching his best form as he left the US Open tied for tenth. That top-ten finish, in turn, led to three further fine performances before he managed to miss the cut yet again – this time in the British Open in July.

But when he left the Wells Fargo earlier that summer, he did not have much time to analyse his fallout, as in the following week The Players Championship hooked up at Ponte Vedra Beach in Florida. A year earlier he had finished runner-up in the event and was celebrating the best moments of his career so far – the win at Wells Fargo and that runner-up spot a week later. But now dismay would follow dismay as he followed up his MDF at the Wells Fargo with an even worse result at the Players. From the highs of second place in 2012, he now missed the cut altogether in 2013.

Even after his first round, Rickie knew that he was definitely not firing on all cylinders. He had always been a realist and his answer to setbacks on the greens had always been to try to see the positives and eliminate the negatives by sheer hard work with demanding practice rounds. But after his first-round seventy-three and a second of seventy-two at the Players, he said he was finding it difficult to hit top form and that he was disappointed with some of his recent efforts. It was suggested to him that he had got off to a start that was neither brilliant nor disastrous – that his golf was sort of middling at the moment. To his credit, he nodded and admitted that was the case, saying, 'It's kind of how this three-week stretch has been for me. Fortunately, I played really well through this period stretch last year; tenth in New Orleans, won in Charlotte and finished second here. I was looking forward to playing and just swinging well. It's like there's cellophane over the hole right now. I can't buy a putt. Obviously, when putts aren't going in, it starts to leak into different parts of the game, and it's really hard to build momentum.'

Was it maybe a mental block he was suffering? No, he said, it wasn't that – it was just that he was making mistakes in minor areas of his game and that was leading to poor outcomes. 'None of it is really mental,' he maintained. 'I'm swinging well and hitting putts where I want to hit them. But sometimes it's just the wrong speed, not reading them correctly and the ball's not going in the hole. It's part of golf – getting through the low spots. I'm looking forward to a week off and then going to Crowne Plaza and then Memorial – places I've played well before.'

Yet there would be no respite at the Crowne Plaza Invitational at Colonial in Fort Worth, Texas, nor at the Memorial in Dublin, Ohio. He finished tied for fifty-fourth at the former and tied for thirty-seventh at the Memorial. As Rickie said, these were venues where he usually performed well. He had particularly fond memories of the Crowne Plaza, where twelve months earlier he had ended the tournament placed tied for fifth – and that uplifting result had come straight after his runner-up spot at the Players. What difference a year had made to his fortunes in the mid-term section of the golfing calendar.

Prior to his first round at Memorial, Rickie said he was looking forward to the event and that he hoped it would be a chance to get back on top form. He once again conceded that he had found it difficult over the last few tournaments but he felt confident that he would soon break through this temporary blockage and start to finish well up the field again. He said, 'I'm definitely excited about this week. I've been struggling the last month-and-a-half so I'm looking forward to being in a good place again. I've made a lot of birdies here before and I've had success in Ohio. I'm just waiting for things to happen.'

It was hardly ideal preparation for the US Open in two weeks' time – Rickie would, no doubt, certainly have preferred hitting the ground running when that Major teed off at Merion Golf Club in Ardmore, Pennsylvania. The plan had been to use events like the Crowne Plaza and Memorial to fine-tune his game; to build upon successes leading up to Merion and then take that good form on to the green when the US Open got underway in the middle of June 2013. As it was, he ended up heading for Pennsylvania struggling to hit top form but working hard to get on top of his game in practice. Analysis was fine but it was putting into practice that which he had found needed changing that really counted. Rickie was a pragmatist and a man who very much believed in action. That was a key part of his make-up – the willingness to work hard and solve setbacks with determined effort. He thrived on positivity and refused to feel sorry for himself when things went wrong.

Rickie was a strong believer in the power of self-belief and that things would eventually change for the better as long as he remained defiant and willing to move forward. And as he headed for the US Open, he had a good feeling that his luck was about to change; that his hard work would pay off – after all, Merion had been the venue when he had been a part of the winning American team in the 2009 Walker Cup. Back then he was still an amateur – now he would return as a professional and he had a gut feeling that he would be successful, finish in the top ten and that it would be the launch pad he needed to chalk up a series of successes after a disappointing set of results. And he would be proved right in both predictions.

CHAPTER THIRTEEN

WE CAN
WORK IT OUT

After that run of poor results in the spring of 2013, Rickie put in the hard hours in a determined attempt to improve his fortunes. He had a two-week break in between wrapping things up at the Memorial in Ohio and heading off to the US Open at Merion in Pennsylvania, so he decided to use the time wisely – he practised hard and long but also allowed himself the occasional rest day to do whatever he wanted. Whether it be simply vegging on the couch, swimming or riding his bike, he made sure he switched off from golf and focused on having a good, relaxing, fun time. It meant that, when he arrived at Ardmore, he was in top condition, mentally, emotionally and physically. He was keen to put his previous disappointing results behind him and make his mark in the second Major of the season – and the second on home soil.

Rickie was well aware that his main rival had won this event in 2011 and that it had launched him into superstardom on the spot and now he aimed to follow in Rory McIlroy's illustrious footsteps. Although he wouldn't quite achieve it, he did finish in the top ten and he left the East Course at Merion with the belief that he was definitely back on track. The event certainly tested Rickie's talent and patience, as rain delayed the start and he and the others were left hanging around idly waiting for conditions to improve. Rickie has lots of patience but, like the other younger golfing stars, did not enjoy this feature of the sport. When the weather turned bad, the problem was that there was nothing to do, except maybe play cards.

They couldn't go outside and have a game of football or drive off somewhere for a couple of hours because the weather could change at any given moment and they could be asked to tee off at any time. So boredom was a problem, especially for the youngsters. For the veterans, it was not as bad – they were well used to this unpredictability and simply sighed and had a coffee and chatted to each other in the clubhouse. Plus this was a tournament with one of the largest number of entrants – in 2013 a total of 156 names were expecting to tee off at Merion – and that number, along with the delay due to the weather, spelt problems.

It was already a logistical nightmare without the rain, as the US PGA decided that the number of golfers due to play should be divided up into fifty-two groups of three. Rickie was grouped with Matteo Manassero and Jason Day and the trio were due out at 8.06 a.m. on the Thursday and 1.36 p.m. on the Friday. But as the first trio would tee off at 6.45 a.m. and 7 a.m. on the two days, it was clear that Rickie and Co. could be among those delayed by the rain, which had poured onto the course for days even before the first round. They were actually thirty-second in line on day one and ended up waiting for their time to come.

Veteran Ernie Els predicted that the conditions could add to the excitement for the fans and that there could be some interesting scores. He also scoffed at suggestions that helicopters could be used to try to dry out the East Course by hovering above the greens. The big South African told reporters:

After the rain this morning, it's going to be very sloppy now. You're not going to see a firm US Open this year, I'm sorry. And I don't care if they get helicopters flying over the fairways, it's not going to dry up.

You're going to see a lot more birdies than ever at US Open venues. Guys who have never played a US Open, they might be lulled into thinking, 'Hey, this is not all that bad.' But I'm playing my twenty-first US Open and I've seen a lot of trouble out there. I think eighteen is a classic great par four. The green is very tough to hit. Most of us will be coming in with a three or four iron. And the way the green is designed, it's on a hill but the green is going away from you on the left side and even on the right side.

And the weather could well make it one of the most competitively fought US Opens in years, added Els. 'I see a very close race with a lot of players in contention this year, unlike other US Opens,' he said. 'It's going to be bunched. It's going to be under par, you'll be seeing quite a few numbers in the red. It's going to be an exciting US Open.'

Golf Digest claimed that the United States Golf Association (USGA) had held an emergency meeting and put in place plans to move the tournament over to the West Course if the East one should prove totally unplayable. There were particular concerns about the eleventh and twelfth holes on the East Course, which had previously suffered flood problems. Matt Shaffer, the Merion director of course operations, told *Golf Digest*, 'It's been flooded probably 40 times in the 12 years I've been here. I've pulled logs and tree trunks off that green. It's had so much silt and grit left on it, the subsurface has turned to concrete. I mean, the players in the U.S. Open better pray it floods a little – otherwise, they won't be able to leave a ball mark.'

USGA executive director Mike Davis had told Shaffer to prepare the West Course for use in case the weather worsened. Davis said he was 'giving the doomsday of all doomsday scenarios' and told *Golf Digest*: 'What if all hell breaks loose? What if it stays flooded for two days? That's why we're going to take some precautionary measures on the West Course.'

Adam Scott, the reigning Masters champion at the time, was one of the favourites to win but even he admitted it would be a difficult task because of the rain. Like Rickie, he also believed in 'practise makes perfect' and revealed that he had been practising for five hours each day in preparation for the tournament. He was glad he had done just that when he was told he would be in a trio with the two main favourites: Tiger Woods and Rory McIlroy.

Also, like Rickie, Scott believed firmly in scouting trips before the event to work out how they might play. 'It's just about trying to soak in as much as you can. I find that that's easier to do out of the tournament week than during the tournament week [because] there's so many distractions out on the course during a practice round that I don't think you're absorbing everything the course is giving to you,' he told reporters. 'So getting rounds in beforehand I think is key, especially for Merion.

'I'm lucky I came up about three weeks ago and played a couple of rounds, so I have seen the course a fair bit. And I've got a fairly good understanding. But I'm a big believer, especially for here, that you have to understand the course very well … I think, for me, the frustrating part at the moment is I'm not getting to hit enough shots off those tees before we start Thursday.'

Of course, the onslaught of the rain made it doubly difficult to prepare for the event, especially as many of the golfers had practised on the East Course when it was not swamped. Indeed, the rain had been falling for a full week before the tournament officially opened and that meant that practice sessions were difficult, if not impossible. That made the decision of golfers like Scott to get in practice rounds a few weeks earlier appear very wise indeed. Some of the participants would be teeing off with no proper chances to have got a feel for the course.

Scott had a feeling that the tournament would still turn out a cracker – perhaps even because of the rain – and he was certainly relishing the opportunity to tackle it with Woods and McIlroy in tow. He said, 'Playing with Woods at any time is always full of energy and electricity. And given the hype around this grouping and it being a Major, it's going to be an intense few days. At some point, if you're playing well and winning a tournament, you're going to have to try and beat Tiger. And that's what you want to be out here for. That's why you spend the hours and test yourself. And I'm looking forward to that Thursday and Friday.'

Rickie had also got in some practice and was as excited as Adam Scott by the prospect of playing an unpredictable course in unpredictable conditions. As well as excitement, he also felt the butterflies of uncertainty in his stomach. He had never been one for overwhelming nerves but this course would provide a yardstick for his season. As he strived to get out of that disappointing run of results, he knew that he needed to make a statement at the US Open. But that would be far less easy in wet, tricky conditions. Any master plan went out of the window: this was now a course where success would most likely be determined by a steady hand and a large dash of luck, rather than mere talent. The victor would be the man who could best conquer the conditions and come home with a steady, sound total.

Rickie finally got on to the course and carded a credible seventy for his first round – an outcome that left him tied for sixth place. The green was soft and tricky after the non-stop rainfall. Given that situation, Rickie declared himself happy with his opening efforts and explained to reporters how the course had, as expected, been difficult to master. 'There's some nasty rough out there,' he said. 'It is short on the card and it was playing soft today.' He admitted he had made mistakes but said he was looking forward to moving forward and improving. Once he had worked his way around and understood how it was playing, he started to believe that he could make a real statement. Rickie said:

I made a few mistakes out there but also some good putts, so it was a little bit up and down. Hopefully, I will be able to avoid making the same mistakes – I missed a couple greens where I shouldn't have and missed a couple short putts.

But other than that, I salvaged a pretty good round out there today. On a Thursday, you can't win an event but you can definitely make a start. I feel like I'm in a good position, swinging well and it's nice to finally see a few putts go in. So I'm excited for the next round – whenever we get to play.

Those final five words of Rickie's quote were arguably the most important – just when would he next walk out on to the green, given the unpredictability of the weather?

In the event, the first round would not be completed on the Thursday. Only those in the morning list – including Rickie and his two comrades-in-arms – completed their rounds. England's Luke Donald made the best stab at it in among those early starters, finishing overnight leader on four-under-par after thirteen rounds. Like Adam Scott, he had scouted the course before the tournament and felt that had paid a dividend for him. He told BBC Sport before the event that he had spent the previous week at the East Course, assessing its greens and working out a plan of attack. He said:

This is a course that has quite a lot of blind tee shots. The greens won't have changed too much in terms of the lines they'll putt so it was good to come here. For the bulk of the players, this is a new place and it's about learning the course, feeling comfortable about it and feeling good about the lines off the tees.

The course will play a lot softer now. The par-fives are very long. I would have loved to have got a little roll off some of those tee shots. It's going to be tough – even the eighteenth, if the wind is into me, is going to be two of my best shots just to get home in two. But any time you get soft greens, it is going to take the edge off some of those short game shots around the greens, so that could be a benefit for me. Sometimes majors are so difficult around the greens then, no matter how good your short game is, you are not going to get it

close. With softer conditions, hopefully touch around
the greens will come more into play.

The round was finally completed on Friday morning, with
Phil Mickelson now top of the leader board thanks to his
brilliant three-under-par round of sixty-seven. Along with
the American ace, only four other players were under par:
Luke Donald and Mathew Goggin at 68 (−2) and Nicolas
Colsaerts and Scotland's Russell Knox at 69 (−1). The top
three players in the world rankings all failed to break par in
the first round – Woods and McIlroy carded 73 (+3) while
Scott posted 72 (+2). The scoring average for the field was
74.31 – more than 4 strokes over par.

That showed the measure of the challenge facing Rickie
and the rest of the stars out there. This would not be a walk
in the park for whoever eventually did triumph: it would go
to the man who best kept his nerve and best worked out a
strategy to conquer the soggy East Course.

The second round started on the Friday and was not
completed until the Saturday as the conditions again dictated
the state of play. At the end of the round, Rickie had dropped
out of the top contenders after carding a disappointing
seventy-six. But a brilliant third round brought him right
back in the running for the title. Rickie left everyone in
his wake with a quite superb sixty-seven. Only Jason Day
had got near him with a fine sixty-eight and he led a group
of just six players to achieve under-par rounds. The round
propelled him right back into the thick of things – he re-

entered the top ten at number nine and would clearly be a contender when the final round teed off.

After that excellent third-round result, Rickie told reporters that the difference between the first and second rounds was simple: he played better and everything he tried came off. He said, 'Everything just seemed to piece together. I played well the first day but had a few holes get away from me. I had a bad stretch but today I made a few putts and kept the round going. I swung it well, drove it a little better and stayed out of the rough as much as possible. Now I'm ready for tomorrow's round.'

He was asked if the fact that he had previously played the course competitively in 2009's Walker Cup had helped his cause. 'It's helped a lot,' he said. 'Just knowing that I've played well here before and that I've made putts here before. The biggest thing this week has just been staying patient, sitting back and letting things happen and I finally was able to do that today.'

He said the course had changed slightly since 2009 and that it played a lot softer and that the rough made it more difficult. And he added:

It's quite a bit different, just with the rough and some of the routing of the fairways and a couple of different bunkers out there. The greens are softer than they were when we played Walker Cup but you add the rough and it's a completely different story. I feel like it played quite a bit easier for us in the Walker Cup. We were able to make quite a few birdies. A lot of us were playing well and, if I would have played the way I did today, then it would have been quite a bit lower. But I'm happy with what happened today.

Rickie always felt he could control it and card a low round and that was exactly what had happened with the sixty-seven that he had achieved to lead the field in the third round.

He was certainly optimistic that he could pull off one of his best-ever results when play resumed for the final round on the Sunday. 'If I can get off to a good start tomorrow, get through the first six holes, stay patient and stay within myself, I can play well from thereon in. I know I'm swinging the club well right now. I've been hitting my lines and hitting a lot of solid golf shots. So if I make sure I'm committed to every shot and put myself in a good position, where I can play the rest of the course the way I have the first three rounds, I'll be OK.'

The bookies doubted that Rickie would win the competition – they had him at 35–1 to do so as the players gathered on the green for the final round. *The Guardian* said he might be worth a punt, arguing that, 'It may or may not be worth pointing out that Webb Simpson won the US Open last year from four back, so a wee punt on, say, Rickie Fowler – who shot a best-of-day 67 yesterday – wouldn't be too reckless a gamble.'

Soon, the time for speculation and talk was over: it was time to walk the walk and, for Phil Mickelson, it would be an unhappy eighteen holes. Mickelson remained at the top of the leader board when the stars teed off on the final day of play. But he ended the day as runner-up, while Rickie finished in the top ten – tied-for-tenth to be precise, as he recorded a final round seventy-four. The tournament winner was England's Justin Rose, who finished with a 1-under-par total of 281. Mickelson was tied for second with Justin Day, with a 3-over-par 283, while Rickie carded a 7-over-par 287.

Rickie had achieved his aim: he was back in the top ten in a tournament – and not just any tournament. He had done it in the second Major of the year. It was a result that really boosted his morale and one that laid down a marker to his young counterparts – that, yes, he was a real contender and, yes, he would be coming after Rory McIlroy some day soon! For the record, Rory finished way down the leader board – thirty-one places beneath Rickie – as he ended fourteen-over-par and tied for forty-first. Even Tiger Woods had failed to keep up with Rickie and the top ten guys, finishing tied for thirty-second at thirteen-over-par.

For the jubilant Rose, it would be his first Major after he completed the tournament without any double-bogeys – a quite remarkable achievement. Rose said, 'It feels fantastic. I committed myself to the process this week. I committed myself to putting a strategy in place that I hoped would work in five to ten years in delivering major championships … it's a moment where you can look back and think childhood dreams have come true.' Rose was the first English player to win the US Open since Tony Jacklin did so in 1970 and the first to win a Major since Nick Faldo claimed the green jacket after winning the Masters in 1996.

For Mickelson, it was more agony and anguish. The perennial bridesmaid at the event had recorded his sixth runner-up finish at the US Open – a record he would gladly have done without. No wonder he was close to tears and devastated as he spoke afterwards, saying, 'This is tough to swallow after coming so close … I felt like this was as good an opportunity I could ask for and to not get it… it hurts.'

But for Rickie Fowler, finishing in the top ten felt like proof that he could do it, that he was one of the best golfers in the world and that he could cut it when the pressure was on after some testing results. Indeed, if anything, as Rickie explained after the tournament, he believed that he could have done even better – that he could and maybe should have finished nearer the top of the leader board.

I didn't finish the round like I wanted to. I felt like I got off to a decent start, made a couple of bogeys but it's understandable on the first six holes. I missed a few putts and didn't close as well as I needed to, making a couple of poor swings coming in. I've been swinging well all week. I saw a lot of positives out of it. And I move on.

You have to be patient at the US Open. It's not one particular shot, it's every shot. You have to give each shot a hundred per cent of your focus and concentration.

But still, all in all, it was a great week and my best finish in an Open.

He had thoroughly enjoyed his few days at Merion and wanted to make the point that he had been treated well and had also enjoyed the challenge the East Course had thrown up after the deluge of rain for days on end. Rickie explained:

I thought it was great being here for the Walker Cup in 2009 and getting a sneak peek at it that week. This week it played different with the rough and some of the fairway routings and the fairways being a little narrower but I thought it was a great test. I think it surprised a lot of people with some of the scores. It didn't play easy out there. It was tricky at times. These greens are old greens but that's where it's fun. It's a shorter course but it's playing long because there [are] certain holes [where] you can't hit [a] driver off the tee. With those shorter holes, they have to put some pins in tricky spots. You put them in the middle of the green, you're making birdies all day long. It's a US Open — it's meant to be a tough test.

It was typical Rickie speak: honest, direct but always positive whatever the outcome, whatever the question, whatever the next challenge. He had made the top ten in a big tournament after something of a barren spell and he had done it in inclement conditions. He had shown determination, commitment, strength and no little talent to do so well when other, allegedly bigger names, like Tiger and Rory had suffered and struggled amidst the hype that follows them at every tournament worldwide.

Rickie was back on track and now the aim was initially to stay there and then to build again and move even further up the rankings. Next up was the Travelers Championship at Cromwell, Connecticut (and another good finish that would serve to further enhance his growing reputation) and then a charity tournament up at Rhode Island Country Club in Barrington. The latter was an event that he liked and would always support given the opportunity. Two events and two opportunities to make a mark and leave a lasting impression. In June 2013 life must certainly have felt good to Rickie Fowler.

CHAPTER FOURTEEN

TRAVELIN' MAN

Escaping the rain and the adulation of his fans at the US Open, Rickie headed off to Cromwell in Connecticut for the Travelers Championship. He was glad to get away from the storms and also glad that Connecticut would give him an even bigger chance than usual to liaise with his army of fans. The Travelers has always been one of the best-attended events on the US PGA circuit, with around 400,000 fans flocking to the course to watch the likes of Rickie in action. Rickie had always been close to his supporters and always had time to chat when he could or to sign autographs. His fans held a special place in his heart and he loved hearing from them and was always grateful for their support, encouragement and good wishes.

After the difficult conditions put paid to any record-breaking rounds at Merion, it was confidently predicted that

Cromwell would offer many more chances to end up below-par and that it would be a much more evenly-contested and competitive event. The website *golfcity.com* reckoned that Rickie was one of the five favourites to triumph at Cromwell – they had him at odds of 18/1 to win and gave the following reasons why he might do just that: 'Rickie shared 10th place at the US Open where he silenced any doubters with a fantastic 67 in the third round, putting him among the best in the field that day. Fowler tied for 13th in his last appearance at TPC River Highlands back in 2010 and is overdue for a win this year.'

Well, he wouldn't get that 'overdue win' but he would once again confirm he was back in business – and back on form – as he repeated his 13th place finish of 2010 up against a powerful field. He posted four rounds of 72, 68, 70 and 64 for a 6-under-par total of 274 and was especially delighted with the second round 68 and fourth round 64. Rickie had spoken with great optimism of his expectations at Cromwell at his press conference to announce his arrival at the tournament when asked how he anticipated it would flesh out after the US Open at Merion. He said:

There is a lot less rough here. I'm excited. The course is in really good shape and it's good to be here after I missed the last two years. It's a little soft from the rain we got yesterday, but it looks healthy and the greens are pretty quick and should firm up for the week and should play well.

There are definitely some tough holes out here. There are a couple of par-4s that are all you want with the long iron in. But other than that, there are definitely a lot more birdie opportunities. Last week you needed to have full focus and full concentration at all times – so that was good preparation for this week. I'm trying to stay in the same frame of mind, making sure I'm ready to hit each shot, commit to it and see where I end up and what I can do this week.

Rickie admitted that he hoped to win at the Travelers – although he knew it would not be easy with a tough field of top-class rivals. He said, 'My main goal would be to be in contention going into Sunday and give myself a chance to win my second Tour tournament.' And he showed how rapidly he was maturing and getting used to the professional circuit and what was required to be a winner as he added, 'I have learned over the years that sometimes the rounds don't go your way, but if you can hang in and try to get the most out of them then you still have a good chance – so they can be the most important rounds. It's very unusual to play four great rounds of golf in a tournament. There is always going to be one tough day.'

They were the words of a man who was coming to terms with the demands of the modern-day golfing era and of a man who was coming to terms with his own game. Here he was, accepting some days would be better than others at different tournaments but also aware that you always stood a chance of glory if you dug in and hung in when things seemed tough and to be going against you. That innate positivity was now being merged with a pragmatism that was the hallmark of a golfer who was heading right to the very top: a golfer who was moving forward through talent, realism and an eminently wise head on young shoulders.

Yes, Rickie was definitely starting to thrive on pressure.

In the event, he walked away from TPC River Highlands 'fairly satisfied' with his tied for thirteenth finish. OK, he hadn't threatened the leaders but his golf had been measured and he had enjoyed the challenge. Ken Duke had waltzed off with the winner's trophy and a cheque for just over $1 million after carding a powerful 12-under-par total of 268 – although he had to keep his nerve to beat Chris Stroud in a play-off. Duke's success proved to Rickie the value of patience and perseverance – qualities he would need in abundance as he continued to try to break through to superstardom with an elusive Major win. At 44, Duke had secured his first triumph on the PGA circuit – not bad for a guy who was ranked 144th in the world. The website *golf.com* summed up just what an achievement Duke's win was, saying, 'Ken Duke needed 187 starts on the PGA Tour to get his first win, securing it at a tournament that is building a reputation for such breakthroughs. The 44-year-old journeyman made a 2½ foot birdie putt on the second play-off hole Sunday to beat Chris Stroud at the Travelers Championship. Stroud, who also was looking for his first title, had chipped in from 51 feet on the 18th hole, to get to 12-under par and force the play-off.'

But Duke made the better approach shot on the second extra hole, bouncing his ball in front of the flag and rolling it close.

At the post-event press conference, a clearly elated Duke admitted that the win meant everything to him. He was one of the circuit's nicest guys and Rickie and the younger elements on the tour didn't begrudge him one bit his moment of sheer joy. Duke said, 'It's been a long time coming. I've been on the Canadian tour, the mini tours, Asian Tour, South American Tour, all of them, Web.com, and it's just great to be a part of this big family on the PGA Tour. Thanks to Travelers for everything they've done, being a big supporter of the tour. It makes it easy for us to come out here and play in beautiful tournaments like this.'

Duke then took time out to explain how he had learned to be patient and to believe that he would break through eventually. He added:

You've got to believe in yourself in everything you do. That's why those guys at the top are winning week-in, week-out because they believe they can do it. It's kind of one of those things once you finally do it it might come easier the next time. And that's how I feel. I owe a lot to Bob Toski, who I met in 2006. He won his first tournament up here in 1953 at Wethersfield and he called me this morning and said, 'It's your time too.' You have to be patient. You can't make things happen out here. You can't win by pushing everything. And that's kind of the way I live life. I'm an easy-going kind of guy, someone who goes with the flow – and that's the way I play golf.

Rickie also enjoyed a laid-back attitude to life and golf, although he had much more passion to win than Duke. They shared the same outlook on success and were both patient enough to know that big wins would come if they remained calm and focused.

After the Travelers, Rickie packed his bag and headed off to Rhode Island Country Club for the Caremark Charity Classic. The event is a professional tournament contested annually as a two-day, two-man team tournament. It features twenty pros from the PGA, LPGA and Champions tours. It is Rhode Island's biggest charity sporting tournament and has raised millions of dollars for local children and families – worthy charitable causes that have always been close to Rickie's heart. Given his altruistic nature, it is hardly surprising that Rickie had insisted on being part of the spectacle. It got more golf under his belt but also allowed him to go a little easier than in a normal PGA tournament.

Having said that, the PGA were keen to trumpet just what it meant to the Caremark Charity Classic to have Rickie and his playing partner Bubba Watson on board. Golf's controlling board in America heralded their participation as 'headliners'. It showed just how far Rickie had actually come in the sport; he was already viewed as one of the golfing heroes who could draw the crowd and who had a realistic chance of success every time he stepped out on the greens. The PGA press release said: 'Headlining the event are PGA TOUR super stars Bubba Watson and Rickie Fowler. Watson, who won the event with partner Camillo Villegas in 2008, returns for his third tournament appearance. This power-house golfer known for his long drives has earned four PGA TOUR victories including the 2012 Masters. Fowler, who has posted three top-ten finishes so far this year, will be playing in the tournament for the second time.'

Pundits also took time out to comment on Rickie's involvement and how it would draw interest in the tournament because of his skills ... and his fashion sense! Paul Kenyon, of the Providence Journal, put it this way:

It will be interesting to see what attraction becomes the No. 1 topic of conversation among fans at this year's CVS Caremark Charity Classic. Will it be Rickie Fowler's clothes? Or will it be Bubba Watson's hovercraft? Odds are that it will be one of the two. The only other item that probably could cause as much buzz would be if Billy Horschel decides to wear the octopus pants he displayed last Sunday in the final round of the U.S. Open. Or maybe if tournament organizers show the Golf Boys Video, in which Watson and Fowler are two of the stars, on the large-screen video boards.

Whatever draws the most attention, it clearly will be something out of the ordinary, something entertaining beyond the on-course work produced at Rhode Island

Country Club by 20 of the world's top players. It is obvious the 15th CVS Classic is no longer your father's staid golf event.

Indeed it wasn't – precisely because of the involvement of stars like Rickie Fowler. Yet while the colourful outfits and young good looks would mean Rickie would be the centre of attention at Rhode Island, he and Bubba would be unable to transfer that into tangible results on the greens. The partnership of Steve Stricker and Bo Van Pelt would seize the day after leading from start to finish. Rickie and Bubba could only finish in fourth place but Rickie was happy enough afterwards; he knew the real focus of the event had been to raise vital cash for charity, not to simply enhance his own growing reputation as a golfer.

He told *GoLocalProv.com* what had inspired him to take part in the tournament for the second successive year, saying, 'We're here for a great cause, we're here to help a few local charities but also to have some fun and play some golf at a great course. The place has a good feel to it. It feels very homey, similar to where I grew up and seems like a fun place to come and hang out.'

And tournament chairwoman Eileen Howard Boone made it clear that Rickie and Co. would certainly be doing their bit for charity as they played some fine golf around the Rhode Island course. 'We're proud to celebrate 15 years of bringing incredible golf to Rhode Island, in support of great community causes,' she said. 'Through the years, the tournament has driven more than $16 million dollars to local charities to help support the vital work they do throughout the region and we're so proud to be a part of such a worthwhile event.'

Rickie had enjoyed the charity event. It was a chance to fine-tune his game in an atmosphere that was less tense and competitive than your normal PGA tournament and, of course, it was a chance to raise funds for those less fortunate than himself. He was definitely one of the most altruistic and compassionate members of the tour although he would wave you aside if you complimented him too much about it. This was a young man who wanted to help because his heart told him he should do – not because of some more complicated ulterior motive. He never saw it as a photo opportunity to be seized with both hands. He would gladly have done it with no publicity at all but, of course, the bigger the publicity the more money one would raise because of increased spectator revenues and TV interest.

After the CVS Classic it was back to business as usual as Rickie now headed off to the AT & T National at Congressional in Bethesda, Maryland. This was the first of three events in which he would play solidly without really threatening to tear up the course and win. He ended as tied-for-21st at the AT & T with a four round total of 283, highlighted by a third day 70.

Then it was off to the UK and the British Open at Muirfield. It was not a happy trip across the Atlantic as Rickie missed the cut with two rounds of 78 and 76. He was not happy with his game and many months later would admit that this was probably his lowest ebb as a professional. It would lead to one major change – he would turn for help to the inspirational Butch Harmon at the start of the 2014 campaign and would admit that the cry for help was as a result of that poor showing at Muirfield. Rickie would say, 'It was just at that point I wanted to have a little bit of guidance and start moving forward. I was kind of at a standstill and wasn't getting what I wanted out of my game.'

So from the low of Muirfield would come a new relationship with Harmon that would drastically improve his form and finishes at the Majors in 2014.

But at the British Open in 2013 Rickie was understandably low and it was even of scant consolation that his number-one rival, Rory McIlroy, also missed the cut. McIlroy, like Rickie, ended 12-over after a 79 on Thursday and a 75 on the Friday. Rickie packed his bags and left Scotland to return to the States. He was determined that he would play his way back into form as he arrived in Akron, Ohio, for the World Golf Championships' Bridgestone Invitational. At the pre-tournament press meeting he admitted that the view of his fellow pros counted for something – that he was happy to have earned their respect and acceptance as a young pro with tremendous potential. Rickie said, 'Once you win an event as a professional, win a PGA Tour event, there's levels of respect.' He was held in high esteem by his rivals but he was wise enough to know that it was still up to him to achieve his potential. If he continued to find his top form difficult to achieve that respect could easily drain away. It was no good having a fine season with some great results if you never reached the same height again.

Rickie knew that he had to continue to keep working hard if he was to reach the next level with his game. For sure, his form in Akron improved upon Muirfield in that he did make the cut and finished tied-for-21st with rounds of 67, 70, 71 and 73. That earned him a cheque for $81,167 but to put it – and his form at that time – into perspective, Tiger Woods pocketed $1,500,000 for winning the event!

He was pleased to have improved on his Muirfield display and that his fans had stuck by him. They continued to mean so much to him as they dressed in similar coloured gear and urged him on from the sidelines. Rickie said, 'I love it when I see them. I saw it all day all 18 holes, so it's fun. Whether I'm having a good day or bad day, I can look over and see the kids running around. It's an easy way to put a smile on your face. I'm lucky to be in the position I'm in, having the fans that I do.'

It was to his credit that he always thanked them for their support and tried to find time for them – whether he was at the top of the leader board or battling to get back to form, as was the case in Akron at the beginning of August 2013. Rickie now headed off to New York to knuckle down on the practice greens in preparation for the final Major of the year, the US PGA championship at Rochester. Again, he would not trouble the guys at the top of the leader board. But, again, he would see a steady improvement in his game as he finished further up the field than he had in Akron – claiming a tied-for-19th place with a one-under-par 279. The hard work was paying off. OK, the steps to the top were small steps but it was better than regression.

And he continued to make headlines and be talked about as America's great golfing hope throughout the tournament. Even before he teed off, there were stories in the press about his game, his composure – and even the gear he was going to wear! For instance, *golfweek.com* did a piece outlining what Rickie would wear each day, saying, 'His signature orange outfit is on tap for Sunday. Fowler will wear AMP Cell Fusion Puma Golf shoes during all four rounds. The pants are called Golf 5 Pocket Tech Pants. He'll wear four different kinds and colors of snapbacks for each of his outfits along with different belts.'

It just went to show the level of interest in the boy – although some grumpy golf watchers made it clear what they thought of the fashion parade. For many, it was an irrelevance to the game itself and would grumble about it even being discussed. What was interesting and of relevance to many of Rickie's uber loyal fans was fodder to others who followed the sport. For instance, Ben in Seattle groaned, 'NOBODY CARES. This business of advanced promotion for these "scripted" outfits interests only the unimportant Golf Fashion Writer. How could Fowler or Watson or Woods getting dressed in the morning even POSSIBLY interest a serious golf fan in any way? Still, I'm sure Puma appreciates the free publicity.'

No doubt that Ben would also not have cared for what another of Rickie's sponsors, Red Bull, got up to, to promote their association with him. The drinks giant set up an indoor driving range with a difference – a so-called 'psychedelic challenge'. Red Bull outlined to the press exactly what Rickie would be up against at the indoor range – it would be: 'filled with mysterious creatures, magical islands, glow-in-the-dark LED golf balls and even a talking moon. The purpose? For Rickie to take down each creature with a tee shot between the eyes – golf training taken to a whole new level.'

For Rickie, it was a day out that was 'fun' and one that he and his long-time caddy Joe Skovron certainly enjoyed. Rickie said, 'We're always looking for new, and sometimes quirky ways to get an edge and Red Bull came up with this fun and inventive animated training challenge. Hitting any type of golf shots where you have to focus on trajectory and distance and trying to hit a certain target can only help you get better.'

Red Bull's press office then outlined how Rickie coped with the challenge, saying, 'His first shot was a 45-yard chip into the centre of a multi-coloured tropical tree. Then he took down a fire-breathing sea monster that sat 56 yards away. Rickie's final target was an oversize trash-talking moon. It was all the great psychedelic impact with no crazy side effects.'

A fortnight later Rickie showed just what he was made of when he put in a fine performance at the Barclays at Liberty National, New Jersey. Our boy finished tied-for-ninth in what was his first top-10 finish in 11 FedExCup Playoffs starts. His second round score of 7-under-par 64 showed just what he could do when all is well. That brilliant round equalled the course record and had analysts and fans purring with delight. It highlighted just how good Rickie Fowler was when playing at his best. After that second-round brilliance, Rickie explained just how he had improved so dramatically after his low point at Muirfield. He said, 'I've been working on my swing and fundamentals. It's all pretty simple. I've been swinging well and hitting a lot of good golf shots – it's nice to see everything working properly.'

Rickie was still smiling and upbeat after the final round. That was down to his improved form and the fact that he and playing partner Jonas Blixt had got together to pull a colourful stunt. They both walked out for the final round in near identical kits – after Rickie had loaned Blixt an identical orange pair of pants and a shirt. They were both giggling like naughty schoolboys as they stepped out of the clubhouse on to the green to tee off. Some of the fans immediately sussed that it was a calculated move – although others seem puzzled and suggested Jonah had dressed that way to put Rickie off his game!

Afterwards Rickie said, 'A lot of people didn't understand that we're actually friends and that this might have been planned. So a lot were saying, "Did you call each other last night?" Well, of course this was planned. He didn't do it to piss me off!'

This was Rickie at his most mischievous and talented.

He had enjoyed playing in the Barclays and having fun with Blixt. The combination of having a good time and playing well would often see Rickie storm up the leader board over the next couple of years. He was no golfing automaton; he was a young man blessed with a rare talent but also a young man who believed that he was lucky to play golf at the highest level. He was determined that he would enjoy it to the full; this was no player who walked around the greens with a long face and tormented appearance. With his emotional make-up Rickie would always have a smile on his face and time for his fans as he moved up the rankings and closed in on his number-one rival, the similarly ebullient Irishman, Rory McIlroy.

Rickie departed from New Jersey in a much perkier mood. He was pleased with his weekend's work at the Barclays and felt he had turned the corner as he continued to battle for more consistency in his play. But a week later Mr Inconsistency had reared his ugly head again as the Boy Wonder managed to miss the cut at the Deutsche Bank Championship. But for many it was no surprise that Rickie had disappointed at the TPC in Boston. As Adam Sarson, on his website *adamsarson.com* pointed out before the event, this was not a lucky stamping ground for Rickie. Sarson said, 'Fowler has never played well here, with his best finish coming in 2010 when he ended up tied for 41st, but much like Rose, his putter has always been an issue. This year though has been a different story, as his putter has been working, despite the fact that he hasn't won a tournament since the Wells Fargo last May. He's finished inside the top-25 in six of his last seven starts, including last week's T9.'

Sarson also offered up the odds on a Rickie victory – they emphasised the size of the task facing Rickie if he were to triumph. The best odds were with Betfair – and it was a massive 61-1 to win the event.

Rickie exited Boston early. He now put in the practice hours to get back on form with his game while also relaxing to ease the stresses. He didn't need telling that on several occasions during 2013 he had failed to live up to his potential: if you missed the cut it was obvious that you needed to work extra hard and put in the long hours. Rickie was always willing and happy to do just that but he still maintained that it was just as important to have fun, too. If he didn't enjoy his golf, then there was even more likelihood that the road back to the top would be still tougher. Work hard but play hard too was Rickie's lifetime motto. He had a life away from the PGA circuit with his friends, family and girlfriend and he valued their feedback and that they offered him a refuge to relax and chill, away from the often high-pressure world of professional golf.

A fortnight later he had swept away the dark cobwebs of that Boston disappointment after spending time with his family and friends. He had also worked hard on his game and was confident that he would put in a much more convincing show at the BMW Championship at the Conway Farms Golf Club in Lake Forest, Illinois. Well, he did just that ... to a point at least as he beat the cut and finished tied for 39th. It was progress but hardly startling progress.

But Rickie never despaired about the inconsistency that had stalled his progress in 2013. He continued to believe in himself and that he would win more tournaments and, eventually, Majors.

He also planned to take part in two more tournaments before the turn of the year – the CIMB Classic and the World Golf Championships' HSBC Champions event. The CIMB was the first event of the new season (after some restructuring by the PGA) and had become a tournament in which the stars of the circuit were keen to participate and even keener to win. And 2013 would be the fourth year of the event but there were changes that helped explain why it had become so popular among the pros. FedEx Cup points could now be won at the Classic, which meant it became the first FedEx Cup event ever played in Asia. It would also the first event ever to be sanctioned by the PGA in South East Asia, and to be played at Kuala Lumpur Gold Club for the first time – and the field had been expanded from 48 to 78 players. There was also the lure of the money – it had a total purse of $7 million and the winner would earn entry to the Masters.

And *golfingindian.com* revealed the partners who would work their way around the lush course – Rickie among them, of course. The website said: 'Another star-studded pairing includes Sergio Garcia, Rickie Fowler and Gaganjeet Bhullar. Garcia makes his first appearance in the CIMB Classic after posting top-10s in two of his last three starts on TOUR. Fowler hasn't played since tying for 39th at the

BMW Championship in mid-September but he did tie for fifth at the 2010 CIMB Classic. India's Bhullar was tied for 10th in this tournament a year ago.'

Rickie himself was more than happy with the pairings – especially as he would be accompanied by Garcia around the course. He had always enjoyed the Spaniard's company and he looked forward to renewing the acquaintance. Rickie arrived in Kuala Lumpur on the Wednesday and spoke at a press conference later that day, admitting he was tired but very much looking forward to taking part. He said, 'It was a long flight but I'm happy to be here. I've been once before to Malaysia and I really like the city and the surrounding area. It's a fun place to come hang out and a nice way to start off the 2014 season.'

He admitted it was 'kind of weird' starting the 2014 season in October 2013 but that he would do his best to get off to a good start, adding, 'Yes, it's a little different starting the year now in October for 2014. But I guess the way to look at it is that we're all out here trying to play well. I'm not really looking at it as the start of the year – I'm just over to play some good golf in Asia. I'm on a three-week trip playing here at CIMB, then HSBC and then going down to Australia for the Aussie PGA.'

In many ways, Rickie's 2013 had mirrored that of his biggest rival, McIlroy. Both young men had been inconsistent as they grappled towards the top of their trade. Did Rickie sympathise with Rory – and did he believe Rory would, like himself, overcome his problems and become more consistent and triumphant? When asked, Rickie nodded and stressed that confidence was a key factor on the path to become a golfing great. Rickie said, 'I think he'll be fine. He's a great player and he's very talented. Golf is a game of confidence. If he gets a few good finishes and gets his momentum and confidence back, he'll be fine. I don't have any worries or doubts about him. He had a tough year last year and golf is a tough game. There's a lot of unanswered questions. You never know what's going to happen the next day, and it was unfortunate to see him struggle a bit. But I'm sure he learned quite a bit from the year and he's going to be stronger moving forward.'

Of course Rickie had more than enough to worry about with his own game than to fret about Rory's too. He vowed to friends and family that he would be going all out for that elusive consistency in the 2014 season. He also made a fair point to pundits when he said that 2013 had hardly been a disaster. Sure, he would have liked a few more wins and top-five finishes – but his 2013 season summary read like this: played in 22 events, finished 3rd in one, five times in the top ten, ten times in the top 25, was 38th in the FedEx Cup standings and had earned almost $2 million for his efforts.

Rickie would finish tied for 19th at the CIMB after carding rounds of 71, 72, 73 and 67. He ended up with a 5-under-par total of 283. The final event of 2013 saw Rickie pitching up in China for the World Golf Championships' HSBC Champions tournament. The planet's top golfers converged on the Sheshan Golf Club in Shanghai for the fourth world golf event of 2013 – and the fifth time it had been held. There were numerous categories for eligibility, but suffice it to say here that Rickie was there because he was in the top fifty of the official world golf rankings.

But he never really threatened to take the field to task, finishing a rather disappointing tied for 55th with a final 1-under-par total of 287. Certainly disappointing when you think that the tournament winner, Rickie's fellow American Dustin Johnson, finished with a 24-under-par total! That was some distance between him and Rickie – 23 strokes, to be precise. Yet Johnson was only two strokes ahead of runner-up and defending champion Ian Poulter with Graeme McDowell another stroke behind. Rory McIlroy, who finished at 15 under, paid tribute to Johnson and the biggest win of his career, saying, 'I don't think anyone could have lived with Dustin this week.'

Rickie left China with the thought of unwinding and enjoying some quality time with his family and friends. The HSBC was his final PGA event of 2013 – but not his final one of the year.

No, he now headed off to Australia and would follow that with an event in Thailand. At the Australian PGA Championship in November he put in a really strong performance that, at one stage, suggested he could even win the event. Rickie carded an opening round 8-under-par 63 to take the lead. He then put in rounds of 72, 71 and 68 to finish just four shots behind eventual winner, Adam Scott. Then, in the middle of December, he carded a second round

6-under-par 66 and a final round 70 to finish tied-for-eighth in the Thailand Golf Championship.

But soon it was time to head home to Florida to indulge in some swimming, some playing on his bike and enjoying some nice food and to relax over the coming holiday season. It had sure been a long year which, for all his laid-back persona and determination to always stay calm and composed, had taken a lot out of him. Certainly, he was very much in need of a good break to recharge his batteries and to rest up. Which is exactly what he planned to do and indeed did – as he caught up with sleep, had fun and generally lived life at a more gentle pace. Like most of the world's top golfers, he used the time between one season and the next to treat himself right – and to catch up with all the family and friends' events he had missed out on during the season.

At Christmas 2013, he also took time out to wish his army of worldwide fans a Merry Christmas and a great holiday season. He took to Instagram to say: 'Merry Christmas everyone, enjoy your day with loved ones, and maybe flip off a house or two?' The flip comment was backed up by a picture of Rickie back-flipping into a swimming pool. At the same time as he relaxed, Rickie was also sometimes dreaming of the year ahead. Would 2014 finally be the year he won a Major – or at least make spectacular steps forward to doing so? By the end of the holiday season, he was raring to go – raring to hit the tour once again and improve upon previous years. And, yes, as it turned out he certainly would make major inroads into winning a Major...

CHAPTER FIFTEEN

SIMPLY MASTERFUL

As the new year of 2014 dawned Rickie told his family and friends in Florida that he felt good and that this could be his best year yet on the PGA circuit. He admitted that 2013 had ultimately proved something of an up-and-down year but, as usual given his positive attitude to life and work, he pointed to certain achievements that showed he had progressed. Sure, he hadn't won a tournament in those twelve months, but his game had improved and he was becoming an all-rounder who could threaten the very best. If he could just iron out the inconsistencies that dogged him during the previous year, he would be rivalling the likes of McIlroy week-in, week-out.

The good news was that he would become a more consistent golfer – par excellence in fact, as he even notched a place in the record books. No, Rickie wouldn't lift a Major, but he came damned close as he competed strongly in them all and made history by becoming the first man to claim top-five finishes in all four Majors since Tiger Woods in 2005. Not only that, he was also only the third player EVER to do so – joining The Tiger in 2000 and 2005 and Jack Nicklaus in 1971 and 1973.

Unfortunately, he was the first player to claim that achievement who also did not win one of those four Majors while finishing in the top five.

But he would come so close, finishing runner-up in two of the five, and third in another. Each year, the boy was getting closer and closer to the promised land of that first elusive Major. His excellent run of form also earned him the right to compete in his second Ryder Cup later in the year.

However the bad news during 2014 was that Rickie's biggest rival, the aforementioned Rory, also stepped up a gear and roared ahead of the whole field as he triumphed in two more Majors. The Irishman's boost in form coincided with him calling off his engagement to tennis star Caroline Wozniacki. Rory's glory didn't deflate Rickie – on the contrary, he was pleased for him as he called him a friend as well as his number-one rival. Rickie was never a spiteful guy; he preferred to see the best in a person and always applauded the successes of his fellow pros.

Even though Rory would claim the glory with his big-hitting wins in 2014, Rickie knew that he himself was ever improving and getting ever closer to the day when it would be him – not Rory – who swept the boards at the Majors.

The beauty of their rivalry was that they were both still only in their mid-twenties and were both still young enough to win trophies galore. Their rivalry and friendship surely had another two decades to take full shape and Rickie reckoned, quite rightly, that meant he had bags of time to catch up with Rory and, hopefully, overtake him as World Number One and the man the others had to beat at the Majors and indeed at every tournament on the Tour.

Having said all that, Rickie got off to a challenging start for 2014 when he struggled to make a real impact in the Humana Challenge and failed to make the cut in three consecutive events! He struggled at the Farmers Insurance, the Waste Management Open and the Northern Trust Open at the end of January and the beginning of February. But being the positive and optimistic guy he is, Rickie refused to let the triple blow get under his skin: no, he did what he always did when confronted by negativity. He practised hard and worked on his concentration; he was a young man who believed in himself and who remained convinced that he had what it took to reach the top, and stay there.

His self-belief would prove key to his development; setbacks were never the end of the road, they merely presented an opportunity to learn and grow. Resolute and intelligent, this was a golfer who would always strive for improvement and who would always put in the hours of extra graft to do so. He loved to play golf and he loved life, too. It was a combination that meant he worked hard but also took time out for fun experiences – riding his bike, chatting with friends and family and generally ensuring he would never experience burnout. Golf was a key part of his life, but it wasn't the only one thing in his life.

And there was another plus-point as he plotted his 2014 campaign. Not long after seeing in the New Year, Rickie revealed that he had made a decision that – as the year unwound – would pay dividends. He brought in Butch Harmon as his swing coach in a definite attempt to move forwards – to have a real go at those Major tournaments. It was 7 January when Rickie officially announced the link-up with Butch – and it made headline news as he had, of course, been working without a coach since the great Barry McDonnell died in April 2011. Rickie headed up to Vegas and was spending time with Butch just days into 2014. 'I've spent a lot of time with Butch and been around with him and with the other guys that he's worked with,' Rickie said. 'He's kind of seen me develop over the last few years and really felt that with the experience he has as a teacher he could help me reach my goals and aspirations and help me be the best player that I can be. It's just basically taking what I have and turning it and cleaning it up and making it the best it can be.'

Butch admitted they had actually been working together since Rickie tied for eighth in Thailand in December 2013. 'We've shared video (since then),' Butch told *GolfDigest. com*. 'He's done good work to clean up things in the swing mechanically. I love the kid. The thing I like is he's been saying, "I want to be known more for my golf than my clothes and my hat. I want to contend in Majors."'

And there, in a nutshell, you had it: that burning desire to compete in Majors and, as the duo settled down in their work, that desire would translate into tangible success.

But not initially, as Rickie struggled in his 2014 debut at the Humana Challenge in partnership with the Clinton Foundation and that trio of missing-the-cut tournaments. Rickie finished tied-for-33rd in the Humana at La Quinta, California. Before the event teed off, he was asked at a press conference what he would see as success for the year ahead. He replied:

> With it being a Ryder Cup year, that's definitely a main goal of mine. Success to me would be going and checking off some goals of mine. Obviously I want to win and then outside that there's four Majors to look forward to. I always knew that it was going to be tough to win on Tour although guys like Tiger and Phil (Mickelson) have made it look a lot easier than it really is. I'm definitely happy with having the one win on the PGA Tour. But moving forward, my goal is to definitely have more than one win in the next four years. It was a great stepping-stone but this year I'm looking to do bigger and better things.

Rickie had got off to an excellent start at the Humana – carding a 68 – and had great hopes of doing well in his home state. He said, 'It was good. I made a lot of good swings, I drove the ball very well today, hit a lot of fairways. I hit some good putts, a couple of bad ones. It's just about getting comfortable. I had a couple of rough swings where I was just a little bit off, made a couple of bogeys, but other than that it was a good solid start, I'm looking forward to tomorrow.'

But he followed up that good round with a 71 and fell down the field.

At the end of February Rickie showed his mettle by finishing third in his fourth consecutive start at the World Golf Championships-Accenture Match Play Championship at Dove Mountain in Arizona. He got off to a flier by defeating Ian Poulter 2 and 1. After his well-earned victory, Rickie said he was delighted with his first opening round win at the event since 2011 and after those three missed cuts during the previous month in 2014. He said:

It's like a mini victory, coming off [the back] of three missed cuts. I've been swinging really well, just not been getting the results. I'm struggling to make putts, which you need to do if you want to make cuts and be in contention. Today I rolled a good one in for an eagle on 13. Obviously it's nice to get a win against anyone but Poulter is probably one of the most well-known match play players. It feels good to be able to move on. It's a big win today but I have a very tough match tomorrow against Jimmy Walker, probably the best player in the world right now, coming off three wins. It's going to be another tough match.

And it would be – but, buoyed by his decent form, Rickie finished 1-up to send Walker packing his bags for home. Rickie was beaming when he spoke of his win, saying, 'To get the win today against Jimmy is nice – he's arguably the best player of the last six months and is on top of his game. I knew coming in today that even if he didn't bring his A game, he was going to be tough to beat. We had a fun match and had a good time out there. It was definitely nice to come out on top.'

On a side-note, Rickie was asked how he would feel about the prospect of representing America in the 2016 Olympics in Rio, if the plan to bring golf back into the fold did indeed materialise. His answer gives another interesting insight into how he ticks – how patriotic a person he is, how much he loves his country and how he enjoys seeing himself as one of a team rather than a solo star. He said, 'It would be awesome, just being a part of the team and being able to represent your country is like nothing else. I've played in two Walker Cups, which is the amateur version of the Ryder Cup, and played the Ryder Cup in 2010. It's so much fun not just on the golf course but off the golf course being around the guys and being a part of the team. You know, playing two years at Oklahoma State were some of the best times of my life. Being able to represent the country, it would be pretty cool to go to the Olympics.'

That was a vision for the future – and a worthy one at that – but for now, his focus was on making further inroads at Dove Mountain after dismissing the efforts of Poulter and

Walker. The third round of the Accenture brought another serious challenger in Sergio Garcia but, once again, Rickie proved himself eminently capable of advancing as he beat the Spaniard 1-up. There would be no easing of the stress in the quarter-finals – every opponent would be top-quality now. So it proved again as Jim Furyk lined up to test Rickie, but Rickie ran out the winner by the same margin as he had beaten Garcia. It was a win that had pushed him to the limits – and he admitted patience and resolve had been as important as simply hitting outstanding shots. His strength of character had helped him cope.

Speaking afterwards, Rickie told reporters:

It was nice to get a win. I played fairly solid and took an early lead, he fought back and I got the lead back. Then Jim got hot from 13 to 16, three birdies and made a good 3 on 16, so I just had to stay patient. I knew he was going to make a charge like that. And I also knew it would be tough for him to continue making birdies. One-down with two to play is not a bad spot to be in in match play and I needed to not worry about the first 16 holes but just go play the last two. With where he hit his second shot on 17, I knew it was going to be tough for him to make four. I played safe on the second shot and got a two-putt to get the win. And it's always nice to go to 18 all square.

It was pointed out to Rickie that for the third straight day he had reached the eighteenth knowing that he needed two good shots to win. He said he was just pleased that he had been able to do just that and was looking forward to the semi-final, which would bring another great player to test him – the redoubtable Justin Day. Rickie also provided a little insight into exactly how he was unwinding away from the greens: at night, he was taking regular walks in the vicinity and enjoying the relaxation. He explained, 'The first night I went on my own, which was fun. I hiked up the hills behind the hotel. My mom and sister came in on Tuesday and I'm going to continue them. I'll be going on a hike a little later this afternoon and just relax and watch the sunset and go down before having some dinner at the hotel.'

Rickie had done brilliantly to reach the semi-final but now his luck would run out as Justin Day proved a bridge too far. Yet that would not be the end of his participation for now he locked horns with the veteran South African Ernie Els in a battle for third and fourth place in the tournament.

Rickie started in scorching form as he led for seven of the first nine holes. But Els is a veteran battler and no way was he going to lie down and die. He forced extra holes but could not reign Rickie in – the boy was determined to get that third place and a birdie on the 19th brought him victory. It was just the boost Rickie needed after an underwhelming start to the 2014 campaign that had led him to fall to 56th place in the world rankings. His victory over Els propelled him back into the top fifty and meant he had qualified for the looming WGC Cadillac Championship at Doral.

'I was kind of planning on it in the beginning of the year and three missed cuts drops you in the world ranking pretty quickly,' Rickie said. 'I knew my game was good – I just hadn't been making cuts. It probably looked a lot worse than it did.'

He reprised his good form at the Shell Houston Open at the start of April, 2014. Rickie's aim with events like the Accenture and the Shell was to fine-tune his game in preparation for the season's first Major, the Masters at Augusta in the middle of that month. He finished 6th at the Shell and was one of only four players to card sub-par rounds at the event in Houston. His rounds of 70-70-68 and 71 meant he had also improved on his two previous performances at the event when he had not been able get below 74 for a round. This highlighted Rickie's progress and the good work he was doing with new coach Butch Harmon.

Midway through the Shell tournament, Rickie spoke about how important a good display in Houston was to his hopes of doing well at the Masters. He said, 'I'm learning each day, really focusing on getting ready for next week. Obviously I want to play well and have a good tournament here and I'm starting to feel comfortable out here and trying to get everything going in the right direction. It's really hard to prepare green-wise for a place like Augusta, but they do a great job here in Houston of getting the course condition-wise set up – with the fairways mowed into the grain and the chipping. It's good prep for next week and I'm excited to be playing well.'

Now Rickie would really make his presence felt at the season's Majors. Sure, he had experienced some disappointing moments – particularly when he missed the cut at those three events in a row – but with the help of new coach Harmon, he was becoming a better player all the time. He was seeing the bigger picture and using events like the Accenture and the Shell as steps towards getting better results at the Majors.

A week after the Shell, he chalked up a tied-for-5th finish at the Masters with rounds of 71-75-67-73. It was his fourth shot at the season's first Major and his display and finish emphasised once again that he was a player who now demanded to be taken as a serious contender. Rickie Fowler was getting ever closer to not just finishing well up the field in a Major, he was becoming the man who could win one. After his first round at Augusta he spoke of the increased confidence he was now feeling: 'I've had some decent finishes here and I've had some good rounds. I think today was a great start. I didn't drive the ball well but I was able to get it around and salvage a decent round of golf. So I really feel like all I can do is go up from here. I'm confident coming off of last week, I feel like I'm swinging well.'

After that third round 67, Rickie was on cloud nine: he really believed that this could be the breakthrough at a Major he had been working so hard to achieve. To go around Augusta five-under-par was no mean feat as Rickie himself acknowledged: 'You definitely feel nerves out there. The juices are flowing; it's Augusta, it's the Masters. It's why I play the game. When I started working with Butch in December, our main goal was to be here contending and having a chance to win the Masters. So, so far, so good. I think tomorrow is going to be something new. I haven't been this close in a Major [to winning]. I finished 10th at the U.S. Open last year, which was awesome and I really feel comfortable on this golf course now.'

He couldn't quite pull off the win – although he had come damned close, entering the final round just two shots off the lead. Yet Rickie knew he had moved forward and, as he departed Augusta for a well-earned week away from the pressures of the green, was becoming ever more confident. Before exiting Augusta, he told reporters, 'I feel great. It's a big step forward for me, especially after all those missed cuts. I've had to grind it out and get on top of my game here. I'm definitely happy and looking forward to a fun week off.'

Yet that old inconsistency would rear its ugly head once again. After a top-notch effort at the Masters, Rickie managed to miss the cut in three of the following five tournaments – and in the other two could only finish tied-for-38th and tied-for-77th. However, he would finally turn his game around just in time – again – for a shot at another Major. The US Open, the second Major of the season, would take place in the middle of June 2014. A week previous, Rickie found form at the FedEx St Jude Classic, tying for 13th with four sound rounds of 70, 68, 68 and 69, ending with a five-under-par total of 275.

To say the return to form was timely would be an understatement. As we say, Rickie is a young man who never suffers from the black dog or negativity, but even he was delighted to have got his game back on track the week before he headed off to Pinehurst, California, for the US Open. In a way, it almost felt as if he were using non-Major events to prepare for the Majors. He had finished tied-for-fifth at the Masters and now came dramatically close to actually winning the US Open. Rickie carded rounds of 70, 70, 67 and 72 to finish on a one-under-par 279. That 67 was a career best round at the event for Rickie and the only under-par round recorded on the day. Rickie was well pleased with this but conceded it had been a slog around the course. He said, 'I'm happy to be under par. It was a grind out there today. I didn't hit it as well as I would like to have. I drove it a little bit poorly and definitely need some work on that tomorrow with Butch [Harmon] before we go out. But I hit a lot of great shots into the greens and I got the ball up-and-down when I needed to.'

Later he would admit that most of his work during the year so far had been aimed at making a success of it at the Majors – and that it would continue for the rest of the year. Rickie said, 'The main goal going into the year was to be ready to play Augusta and be ready for the Majors – and to contend in the Majors. I really wouldn't care about what happened in the other tournaments because my main goals were to be ready for the Majors. I put myself in that position at Augusta and I've done that this week. So I would definitely be very happy at the end of the year if I had been in contention at all four Majors.'

So there you had it … as we had suspected, the missing

cuts and disappointing results at earlier tournaments was all part of a grand master plan. What mattered to Rickie was moving on to bigger dreams – to not only competing well at the Majors but actually being in a position to win them. Rickie's playing partner on the final round of the US Open was Martin Kaymer, who would go on to win the tournament. Rickie clearly meant business now as he pushed Kaymer all the way with a final-round, 2-over 72 to finish tied-for-second with Erik Compton. It was Rickie's best finish at a Major and he pocketed $789,330 for his efforts. It was also the sixth runner-up finish and his best performance in six US Opens (his previous-best was tied-for-10th in 2013).

And his pairing with Kaymer, 29, produced another interesting fact – as the PGA pointed out, it was just the third final grouping at the US Open since 1965 with two players in their twenties. The others were John Mahaffey (28) and Jerry Pate (22) in 1976 and Woods (26) and Sergio Garcia (22) in 2002.

Later Rickie told reporters how happy he was to have finished runner-up – and repeated the mantra that it had been part of his plan to do the business at Majors. He said:

I'm really happy about it. Goals going into the year were to get ready for Augusta and then contend at Majors. Finishing tied for fifth and tied second here in the first two Majors of the year, I'm definitely pleased about that and looking forward to the next two. I felt really comfortable here, which is a very good thing. I've only played in a handful of final groups – this was my first one in a Major. The more experience you can get in the final groups, and especially in Majors, it definitely helps. With the way I kind of handled myself and kept going through the process on each shot, there was only a handful of shots this week that I wasn't really prepared to hit and hit them without being ready to hit. So definitely take a lot away from this week and the pairing today as well.

He was asked if his fine display answered the pundits who criticised him for not having more wins under his belt. Rickie answered, 'It doesn't matter what I do, I'm always going to have critics. I'm not really worried about them. I have so many more people that are fans and awesome people in the media that take care of me and write great stories – and I'm just going to keep playing well and keep moving forward. Obviously there's been some great finishes, but I want to win and I want to win more.'

And had Rickie noted how he seemed to give his best rounds on the Saturdays at the Majors? He had, after all, shot a 67 here and at the Masters on that day of the week. He laughed as he said, 'I guess my mom and sister's cooking has been good. I've got to check and see what we've been eating on Friday night. What was it? Yeah, it was a good meal Friday night. I'm not going to give it away. I don't think I've had very good Saturdays outside of Majors but I'm happy that

I'm playing better in Majors than regular events. I would rather play well in Majors – it's a good thing.'

But could he go the extra step-up from runner-up at a Major to winning one? I have no doubt that the answer to that is in the affirmative and his performances at the remaining two Majors of 2014 would go to show that Rickie Fowler was indeed ever closing in on that first Major crown.

CHAPTER SIXTEEN

A MAJOR CONTENDER

Those top five finishes at the Masters and the US Open gave Rickie a definite lift. All his planning and all his efforts over the previous nine months had been aimed at contending in the four Majors during the season and leaving Augusta with a fifth-place finish, and Pinehurst as a runner-up served only to show that, yes, his blueprint was correct: by using the smaller tournaments to fine-tune his golf, he was ready and able when the Majors came around. Now, as the summer of 2014 loomed, the big question was, could he continue his success for the remaining two Majors of the year?

Well, we didn't have to wait long to find out as the British Open was next up – just a month after the US Open, in fact.

Considering how impressive Rickie had looked at the Masters and the US Open, it was something of a surprise that he was rated as a 25-1 shot to lift the British Open trophy at Hoylake. But the guys behind the Betting Directory realised he was going to come a lot closer than that. They made their case for him to be considered as one of the top contenders, saying, 'Fowler was hugely impressive at the Open Championship in 2011 as he finished tied fifth after coping with testing weather conditions at Royal St George's. He has continued to improve and he is arguably a man for the big occasion, as he showed earlier during 2014 when top-fiving at both the US Masters and US Open.'

And Irish bookmakers Paddy Power made clear they believed that Rickie COULD win the Open – by making him one of their seven top tips to do just that. They said:

There'll be no danger of not spotting the tangerined-one if he's contesting Paddy Power's seven places come Sunday on Merseyside. Fowler's switch to swing coach Butch Harmon seems to be paying dividends and can build on his four-year form figures of 14-5-31-MC (missed cut) heading to Royal Liverpool. Team Fowler decided to concentrate on being around for the awkward interviews at the end of the Majors this year and it's paid dividends so far. Posted a T5 behind Golf Boys side-kick Bubba Watson at the Masters and T2 at the US Open while a final-round 65 to finish T8 in Scotland will have oiled his engine for this week's test, after being involved in a minor car crash two weeks ago. Still just the one PGA Tour win since 2008 though – the Wells Fargo Championship in 2012.

As Paddy Power pointed out, Rickie did warm up for the Open by heading north to the Scottish Open the week before he would tee off at Hoylake. It proved to be a journey worth making as Rickie finished tied-for-8th in the far north of the country at Aberdeen. He was the highest American finisher (Phil Mickelson was next in line at tied-for-11th). Mickelson had triumphed at the tournament the previous year and it reflects well on Rickie that he finished above the ex-champ. *GolfDigest.com* picked up on the fact that Rickie was becoming a player who loved the spotlight and the bigger the event, the better. They perceptively commented: 'More and more it would seem, Rickie Fowler is a man for the big – or biggest – occasions. And, while he likely isn't going to win the Aberdeen Asset Management Scottish Open tomorrow, Fowler has done much to enhance his already substantial reputation … All of which augurs well for next week, when the oldest of the four major championships returns to Hoylake for the first time since 2006.'

Rickie told reporters of his affection for links courses and that he believed his experiences in Aberdeen would indeed stand him in good stead for the British Open at Hoylake. He said:

I just love links golf, especially hitting shots back into the wind. Downwind is fun, but playing the opposite way is better. You have to hit the ball in the middle of face and control the flight of the ball. That's not quite the norm on tour. We play in windy conditions obviously – and the greens are firm on the PGA Tour – but the air over here is heavier and affects the ball a lot more.

I don't know if that adds up to a harder question than we see most weeks, but I enjoy the challenge of it. I'll definitely be back for more.

It was suggested to him that he might have been better off taking a week away from competitive golf before Hoylake – as some big name players did. He disagreed, saying, 'I played for three weeks before the US Open and managed to finish second there. So I don't think it is asking too much of myself to play here. I feel like this is a good way to find out where I'm at heading into Hoylake. I've been able to see the areas of the game I need to work on, my long irons off the tee for example.'

He had enjoyed a good workout up in Scotland and consequently travelled back down to England in good spirits as the countdown began to the British Open at Hoylake. Sky Sports predicted that Rickie was a contender who could not be discarded when the young man arrived for practice on the Wednesday before the event teed off. They said, 'Rickie Fowler, just as he's done ahead of excellent performances in the first two majors of 2014, has warmed up well with a strong performance (a top 10 in Scotland). That suggests he's discovered the art of peaking.'

That struck me as a most perceptive analysis – the idea that, yes, Rickie had planned his whole season around the four Majors and that he had peaked when they teed off.

That had been the case at the US Open and it would be repeated at Royal Liverpool in mid-July. Rickie would start off well and progress even better after getting to grips with the course on the Thursday. He carded four rounds of 69, 69, 68 and 67, to finish with a fantastic 15-under-par 273 total. It meant he had repeated his runner-up spot from the US Open – and proved once and for all that he was a golfer who was going to the very top, a golfer who was on the brink of greatness and only tiny details away from scooping that first Major trophy. Rickie would end up tied-for-second with Sergio Garcia – and no prizes for guessing who waltzed off with the trophy. Yes, his nemesis but friend, Rory McIlroy. Just as Rickie had stepped up his game during the first six months of 2014, so had the Northern Irishman.

The previous year both had not lived up to the absolute peak levels we knew they were capable of but now they mirrored each other in a more positive way by stealing the honours at Royal Liverpool. Rory triumphed with a final round of 71, which gave him a 17-under-par total of 271. He finished two strokes clear of Rickie and Sergio and also made the record books by becoming only the third golfer to lift three of the four Major titles by the age of twenty-five (joining Woods and Nicklaus on that remarkable plateau). Two strokes – that, in essence, summed up the gap between Rickie and Rory. A small gap that was being challenged by Rickie all the time – he knew that if he kept up the good work he would surely overtake Rory, turning the small gap into a win. Rickie would keep plugging away, desperate to notch that first Major and to prove he should indeed be considered as McIlroy's main rival.

The British Open has always been legendary for its particular demands – whether staged at Hoylake, St Andrews in Scotland or Sandwich in Kent. Those demands usually centred around inclement weather, with rain and strong winds a constant test. Royal Hoylake in 2014 would prove no exception to that rule – Royal Liverpool Golf Club was located in the town of Hoylake on the Wirral peninsula. The golf course bestrides Hoylake and another town, West Kirby. Near the seaside, the eighteen-hole course has always been victim to the winds and rain that roll in from the water. The Open was being held there for the first time since 2006 – and that tournament was the first on the course since 1967, which showed it was finally, if still only periodically, coming back into fashion as a venue for the biggest event on British soil.

The official website of the Open – appropriately called *theopen.com* – helpfully provided its own background information for the press before Hoylake. The information was enlightening in explaining the historical significance of the course – and just why it had come back into fashion as a location for the Open. It said:

Royal Liverpool – or Hoylake, as it is usually known – is the second-oldest seaside links golf course in England. Built on the racecourse of the Liverpool Hunt Club, it retained a dual role as horse-racing venue and golf course for the first few years of its life.

Two of the three amateurs who have won The Open were Hoylake members: John Ball and Harold Hilton. The other amateur winner, Bobby Jones, won his third Open at Hoylake, an event which was the second of four steps in his unmatched Grand Slam. Aside from Hilton and Jones, Hoylake has witnessed a string of unique Open winners:

Arnaud Massey became the only Frenchman to win the title in 1907; Fred Daly became the first Irishman to do so, in 1947, and Argentinian Roberto De Vicenzo became the first South American to win a Major in 1967.

In 2006, following years of work undertaken to create the space needed for a modern Open, the event returned to Hoylake. Tiger Woods produced an imperious display of intelligent golf that would ensure a second Open victory in as many years. In 2014, Rory McIlroy held off Sergio Garcia and Rickie Fowler to win his first Open and third Major title.

Rickie will no doubt be happy to know his efforts at Hoylake in 2014 meant he had finally made it onto the history pages of the Open – along with Rory and Sergio.

Back in 2006, it had defied its traditional stormy weather as the heat steamed down on the course during an extremely hot summer. That would provide the cue for a still dominant Tiger Woods to roar to his third Claret Jug win on a course that was hard and conditions that were testing only for the heat – the golfers were spared the traditional wet, stormy weather that has contributed to the myriad surprising successes and failings at the British Open over the years.

Sky Sports' golfing pundit, Colin Montgomerie, predicted that Hoylake in 2014 would most likely provide a real test for the golfing greats who descended upon it. He said:

There is a bit of mystery about the place. It is a pretty unknown course and those who didn't play there in 2006, primarily the guys under 30, will face a new test. I wouldn't say it has the most character, as that's Turnberry, and I wouldn't say it's the toughest, as that's Carnoustie, but it is a very strong test of golf.

It is a very underrated course – but if you underrate it, you will be punished.

It looks pretty benign and not particularly demanding so people could fall into the trap of thinking, 'This isn't that tough' – and then find themselves four or five-over par very quickly.

But after his first round 69, Rickie told reporters he actually enjoyed playing in testing conditions. He said, 'I definitely enjoy playing in the wind. Sometimes you can use the wind to your advantage if you know how to play it properly. So that's why I enjoy playing here. I feel like I can control my ball out in the wind. Whatever the weather does or decides to do, we'll be ready to play.'

He also claimed the conditions were hardly anything new as he had played in similar circumstances back home, saying, 'Back when I grew up in Southern California it usually blew a lot every afternoon. I did play a lot in the wind. And then at school in Oklahoma, there were a lot of days where it blew hard. I'm not a stranger to playing in cold, windy weather.'

Rickie stressed once again that he felt confident his approach to the tournament had been near perfect; that taking time off and only playing in the Scottish Open was ideal preparation. He had unwound and relaxed for a few weeks and then got back into the swing of things up in Aberdeen. 'I had three weeks off, so I was able to relax and get ready for the two weeks over here,' he explained. 'The biggest thing was getting over and playing the Scottish, and seeing where my game was at. I shook off a few things the first couple days up there. It was a chance to build some confidence with a good solid finish. The round I had on Sunday [in Scotland] definitely gave me some confidence going into this week.'

The boy had done good with that 69 – he was in contention with playing partner Garcia – but he wasn't the pacesetter. No, McIlroy was determined to steal the duo's thunder and did just that with a brilliant 6-under-par first round of 66. Rory told the press that it meant a lot to him – that it had always been his dream to win the British Open and that he was delighted to have taken a strong first step to doing just that. He said, 'Anytime you shoot 66 at the Open Championship, you're going to be pleased. We had perfect scoring conditions out there this morning. There wasn't much wind early on. The wind started to pick up a little bit on the back nine. But, yeah, there was plenty of opportunities to make birdies. I was able to take a few of them. Another great start and I am looking forward to getting back out there tomorrow.'

It was suggested to Rory that he might not look forward to it as much when he learned the forecast was for rain and wind. He laughed that off – just as Rickie had – and made the point that his exploits at the Scottish Open in Aberdeen had prepared him well for such conditions – just as Rickie did. Rory added:

I am glad that I went up to Aberdeen last week and played under some different conditions. I thought that it might prepare me well for this week. I've seen that there could be some weather moving in tomorrow afternoon and high winds and maybe a bit of rain and a couple of thunderstorms. But I feel like I'm well prepared this week for whatever the conditions.

I've practised in windy conditions the last few weeks. I've practised the shots that I might need for a bad day like tomorrow might be. Will that help in any way? It might do, because you're really just concentrating on one shot at a time when the weather is like that. It's not like I've shot good scores in first rounds and haven't backed them up before. I'm used to doing that. I just haven't done it recently. We'll see what tomorrow brings and what weather it is and try and handle it as best I can.

As statements of intent went, it certainly gave Rickie something to chew over. Like himself, McIlroy hadn't come to the North West of England to see the sights. He was deadly serious in his determination to chalk up his first British Open win – and if Rickie wanted to beat him to it, he would clearly need to put in three remarkable rounds, starting on the Friday. Even after his confident opening 69 he trailed Rory by three strokes and the Northern Irishman was going to take some stopping if he kept up that pace over the three remaining days.

After another confident round on the Friday, Rickie carded a second 69. But would that be enough to draw him closer to Rory? Rickie had high hopes of closing the gap because Rory had constantly fluffed his lines on what came to be known as his 'Freakish Fridays'. Even at the Scottish Open, McIlroy had shot a brilliant first round of 64 – which was a new course record – but then imploded in the second round, carding a 7-over-par 78. The *Golf Channel* examined the stats and found that at 13 stroke-play events during the season, Rory had failed to hit under 70 nine times in the second round and his average stood at 72.2 on those 'Freakish Fridays'.

Rickie hoped that Rory might suffer more jitters as they teed off on the Friday, but this time Rory was not going to let himself be jinxed. Before teeing off, he was honest enough to admit that, yes, he had suffered setbacks on certain Fridays but denied that it had become something of a mental jinx and that he was particularly worried by it. 'I had a bad

Friday afternoon at Augusta and then just made the cut,' he said. 'And then I started off horrifically at Quail Hollow on Friday afternoon. And then did the same thing at Sawgrass. That's three tournaments in a row. But there's nothing really to it. It's just about maybe having higher expectations going out on a Friday because you shot a low round [the previous day], and just trying to put those expectations aside and trying to take it one hole at a time.'

Unfortunately for Rickie, Rory stormed to another superb round of 66 – a score that put him even further ahead of the chasing pack. He was now 12-under-par and led the Open by four shots, with Dustin Johnson his leading challenger. Rickie – who had been hoping to close the gap on his rival – now found himself six shots adrift. Rory was later once again asked about the 'Freaky Friday' curse and laughed it off, pointing to the brilliant round he had just completed. 'I think you guys were making a bigger deal out of it than I was,' he told BBC Radio 5. 'But, yeah, I played really well. Overall, another, really, really good day.'

Indeed it was, but not for Rickie. Yet he refused to be downhearted, saying it was all still to play for and that he believed he could improve and narrow the gap. 'All in all, it's been a great start for the first two days,' Rickie said. 'I definitely feel like I can improve on the first two days. I left a little bit out there. Today I didn't feel great with the putter. My eyes were a bit off, but it was a good, solid round. I'm excited for the weekend see if we can get a few things ironed out and keep moving forward.'

He told reporters that he often had to go carefully when he had trouble with his eyes, saying:

I probably slept on the wrong side. My eyes are very sensitive. I struggle with some of the set-up things sometimes – my hips get open, my shoulders get shut and my head gets behind the ball. If any of those are just a little off, and my head is not in the proper position, then my eyes aren't able to see the line properly. So I usually use an EyeLine putting device, which has a mirror. I'm able to check everything there. I'll just use that to go through a checklist and see where everything is at. And typically it's a pretty easy, quick fix. But if one little thing is off, it can throw off your eyes.

It gave us an intriguing insight into a behind-the-scenes problem that other golfers have admitted to suffering from – and to know that you could buy a readily-available device to help surmount the problem. Certainly it was clear that it would take much more than a troublesome eye for Rickie to wave the white flag of surrender to McIlroy. Having said that, Rickie was still happy to praise the Irishman's talents – and admit that he did hope the weather could cut him down to size! Rickie said, 'When his driver is on, he's almost unstoppable. I know he gets a little off here and there and that there's been a couple of Fridays where he's struggled a little bit and fallen back. But he's not scared to go and keep going. So if he's playing the way he is right now and keeps playing through the weekend, he's definitely going to be tough to catch. But weather could throw in a little mix there tomorrow!'

This was typical Rickie – honest to a tee and never giving up the ghost. Admitting Rory would take some stopping, but refusing to simply give up and accept second best. Unfortunately, McIlroy was in one of those moods when there was no stopping him. For the third successive day at Hoylake, he left Rickie and Co. in his wake.

The weather had been threatening to get worse as the Open unravelled, and Rory had to contend with a downpour and the threat posed by the ever-improving Rickie. The Irishman managed to do both and extended his lead to six shots with a round of 68. The BBC pointed out that this was 'the biggest final-day advantage at the Open since Tiger Woods led by six in 2000'. Behind Rickie, Sergio Garcia and Dustin Johnson were tied for third, at nine-under-par.

Rory spoke of how he had remained focused and of how he again felt 'comfortable' in pole position. He said, 'Yes, I'm comfortable leading the tournament and with my golf game and on the greens. This is the third night in a row that I'll sleep on the lead! It helps that I've been in this position before and I've been able to get the job done. I just need to go out there tomorrow and play one more solid round and hopefully that'll be enough.'

Rickie also carded a 68 to match Rory, but still trailed him because of the latter's scorching opening two rounds. Rickie declared himself more than happy with his form and his round but admitted that Rory was pulling away. He said, 'I'm definitely satisfied with my game. I got off to a great start today through 12 holes. I was playing very solidly and looking to draw on that tomorrow. I had two tee shots that slipped away from me a little bit on the back nine and one approach shot on 17. Three of those definitely cost me the three shots coming in. If I'm able to get off to a good start tomorrow maybe I can put a little bit of pressure on him – because he's definitely in control of the tournament right now.'

The American golfer did put the pressure on but the boy from Holywood was equal to it. Rory won his third Major crown at just 25 by two shots from Rickie and Sergio, who both kept up the pressure throughout the final day. It was no disgrace at all to finish tied-for-second in another Major.

Rory's final round 71 and a 17-under-par total earned him the right to carry off the Claret Jug. It was a round that certainly tested him to the full with Rickie and Sergio constantly threatening to close in on him. Rory passed the test with an assurance and authority that belied his tender years. The victory also moved him up from being ranked eighth in the world to second. It also meant he now needed only to triumph at the scene of his greatest upset – The Masters in Augusta – to complete a career Grand Slam.

After his triumph Rory rushed over to hug his mum, Rosie, and his dad, Gerry. This was the first Major win by her son she had attended and Rory would later explain how he felt and how much the win meant to him. 'It feels absolutely incredible. It's cool that they put your name on there even before you get it. So that was a nice little touch. I'm happy I gave myself enough of a cushion today, because there was a lot of guys coming at me, especially Sergio and Rickie. It obviously hasn't sunk in yet. I'm going to enjoy it and let it sink in tonight in the company of my friends and family.'

For Rickie there was no despondency. He had done well – very well – and had run close to winning a Major. He had now started to make a habit of finishing runner-up in Majors and that gave him much confidence and something concrete to build on, as he told reporters after the contest had ended. He was also extremely complimentary about the skills of Rory, saying:

It was a great back nine but I didn't get off to the start I really wanted to. With the way the front nine was playing, there were a couple of holes that were downwind and that had a chance to get some birdies going. I wasn't able to do that but I'm pleased with the way I hung in there – the way I fought it out. I made some great par saves. I tried to give Rory a little run at the end, but just got on the gas a little too late.

It was a great week at the US Open – and here too. Rory just kind of distanced himself from the field a bit, especially with his finish yesterday. It's hard to be disappointed because it was such a great week. And with the way I had been playing in the Majors, there was some pressure to play well this week. But I've felt comfortable and it doesn't feel like a big stage. It feels like I should be here and there's plenty more to come. I'll take 15-under in a lot of Majors and sit there and wait in the clubhouse. Congratulations to Rory. He played awesome.

Once again, in the face of what must have been hard to take after finishing with such a remarkable score, Rickie showed his humanity and his humility. There is little doubt that when he does land that first Major, Rory and the other top young guns on the circuit will cheer for Rickie and offer him their sincere congratulations. He was a credit to himself and a credit to the game of golf. He was well liked, well respected and widely admired on the circuit. In fact, Rickie Fowler was one of the most popular guys in pro golf because he never bad-mouthed his rivals and he never moaned or groaned.

Indeed his final comments to the press summed up his honesty and why he was such a likeable guy, as he praised Rory and a couple of other legendary figures, also conceding that Rory would now take some stopping. 'Rory is obviously doing well with three Majors now,' Rickie said. 'I definitely have some catching up to do but I am getting closer. It's been fun to be in contention at the Majors this year. As far as changing of the guard, I don't see Tiger and Phil and some of those guys running off anywhere. We're ready to go to battle against them, though.'

Did he think Rory would now go on to complete his Majors collection with a win at the Masters? 'I really don't have any doubt that he'll win there,' he said, smiling. 'But it would be nice if I can get there first!'

For now, he would leave England with fond memories and more belief than ever that he was on the right track – that he had indeed made the right decision to concentrate on the Majors at the expense of other tournaments in 2014. Rickie now turned his focus on the final Major of the year: the US PGA tournament in Louisville, Kentucky, when he and Rory would once again be going head to head for glory. He had just a fortnight's grace to prepare for the tournament and to arrive in good shape both physically and mentally.

Rickie spent the time profitably, fine-tuning his game with more practice but also ensuring he unwound too. All work and no play would make Rickie a dull boy – he was wise and mature enough to know that he needed to find a balance between work and leisure. And he had done just that as his career evolved. The proof of the pudding lay in the eating – or the progress in the Majors in Rickie's case. After pushing McIlroy so closely at the British Open, he now did the same in the US PGA at a rain-soaked Valhalla Golf Club.

Rory, Rickie, Phil Mickelson and Henrik Stenson duelled for glory despite the depressing weather conditions. Once again, it would be the Northern Irishman who would triumph, lifting his second consecutive Major crown in less than a month. McIlroy was clearly now the man to beat if Rickie was to lift his first Major. Rory finished at a remarkable 16-under-par given the inclement conditions, carding a four round total of 268. Mickelson was the runner-up, just one stroke behind while Rickie tied-for-third with Stenson, two strokes adrift of McIlroy.

Rickie had done well again in another Major but there was talk among the press pack – and on the greens – that he might even have pulled off his debut win as he led the field for much of the final day's play. But as darkness fell, so did Rickie as he struggled to maintain his exhilarating form.

He would admit later that he was gutted not to have won – he felt he had a genuine chance to lift the trophy, even more than when he had finished second at the British Open. Rickie would admit:

It was a little different playing the last few holes in the dark. I just wish I could have done better on the last couple of holes. This is probably the one that hurts the most for me with the Majors this year. The first three were a lot of fun and obviously I was in great positions and had great finishes. Today I felt like I could go out and win it. I had put myself in a good position – but the back nine wasn't what I was wanting. But looking back on the year, it was pretty awesome through the Majors and something I can be proud of.

Rickie had also explained how he had continued his mission to do well in the Majors right up to this final one of 2014. He said, 'The week before the Majors has been big for me as far as going through a bit of a checklist, putting myself in a position where I'm in competition and I have to hit certain golf shots, whether it's tee shots, approach shots, getting balls up and down, putts, to make sure that I'm doing everything how I want to be, starting the ball on line in any situation. If I'm starting the ball where I want to.' He confirmed he had stuck to the checklist at every Major that year and that it had given him the confidence to believe that he COULD win one. Certainly, the year had been a success in terms of his performances at the four Majors – he had come a long way, as his finishes in those tournaments confirmed. He was on the brink of winning one and it would surely now happen sooner rather than later.

The season had given him hope – and now he would work along the same lines into 2015. He had notched ten top-10 finishes during the 2013–14 PGA Tour season and he had one final hurrah in the campaign. Rickie would finish eighth at the Tour Championship event in mid-September and that would earn him a top-10 spot in the world rankings. He had enjoyed the challenge of the Tour Championship in Atlanta, Georgia, where he posted rounds of 69, 68, 67 and 71 and finished on a five-under-par count of 275.

Rickie later agreed that he had advanced dramatically as a player and a contender over the last twelve months.

When asked which tournament he felt had been his best in terms of almost but not quite finishing victorious, he was once again emphatic in pointing to the US PGA – although he admitted he was proud of his work at all four Majors in 2014. Rickie said, 'Augusta was always going to be a bit of an outside shot. I still wasn't 100 per cent comfortable as far as being in contention. I felt great at the US Open and I was in a great position in the PGA. I really felt like I could win that tournament. I felt like I was very in control of my golf game but then, unfortunately, just didn't get the ball close enough on the back nine there to make any birdies.'

Throughout the season, Rickie had also regularly made it clear that he had two key aims he wanted desperately to achieve in 2014. The first was to be in contention at the Majors – and he had certainly ticked that box. And the second was to be part of the Ryder Cup and to be on the winning side. Well, he would achieve the first part of that when he was chosen to be part of the Team America squad who travelled with great hopes to Gleneagles in Scotland for the 40th Ryder Cup tournament against the Europeans.

But the second part of the dream was unattainable as the powerful hosts retained the trophy with an emphatic 16½ points to 11½ win. Rickie had made headlines in the UK by turning up for the event with the letters USA cut into his hair! He admitted he had been taken by surprise by the reaction to his haircut, saying, 'It's gone a bit crazier than I expected. Just thought I would do it for a little team spirit and knew the guys on the team would like it. It's been fun to see the reaction of the fans and people, social media, guys on the European squad and caddies over there, as well.'

But some pundits had claimed it was a sign of brashness and an eagerness to hog the limelight – which I would never say were characteristics of Rickie's. OK, he always wore orange on the last day of tournaments and he was involved in numerous kit and gear sponsorships. But he never did things simply to draw attention to himself – it was all part of his pride in himself, his university and his county and country. As he explained, saying, 'I'm just myself. I'm not trying to be anyone else. I'm not trying to fit in any particular way. It's just me being me. I'm not trying to hurt anyone's feelings – I'm just proud to be from the USA and be over here playing The Ryder Cup Team. If people take it the wrong way, it's too bad for them. It's unfortunate. You've got to show some patriotism and spirit for your country. Like I say, I'm excited and it's going to be a fun week.'

Unfortunately, that flamboyance and spirit off the greens was not matched on the greens. He and partner Jimmy Walker got off to a steady start by halving their Friday four-balls encounter with Thomas Bjorn and Martin Kaymer. The same duo then earned the same result against McIlroy and Garcia in the afternoon's foursomes.

Walker and Rickie then also halved their Saturday fourballs clash with McIlroy and Ian Poulter. But they lost 5 and 4 to Graeme McDowell and Victor Dubuisson in the afternoon foursomes.

Rickie's participation in the tournament would end with a further loss on Sunday as he fell victim to the brilliance of old foe McIlroy, losing 5 and 4 in the singles. All in all, it was not the best of team tournaments for Rickie. He and his US teammates were quick to congratulate the victorious Europeans but there remained the feeling that they could maybe have put up a better fight. The result was emphatic and hard to stomach for a nation so proud of its golfing heritage as the United States.

Rickie would admit he was disappointed but, as always, saw the result with the glass half full, rather than half empty. He had enjoyed taking part and the camaraderie with his teammates, saying, 'These are weeks that I don't want to miss, win or lose. The time that you get to spend with 11 other guys on the team and the captains, it's a special week. It would be nice to get a win one day soon but it's a special week.'

And that, in a nutshell, sums up why Rickie is a special guy. A brilliantly talented golfer who is on the brink of Major success and a young man who always tries to see the positives in golf and life. A young man who counts his blessings every day and who is a fine example of the American dream come true.

Now let's wrap up this biography with a final, in-depth analysis of Rickie's rivalry with Rory McIlroy – the remarkable ever-developing duel that will surely define golfing legend for decades to come.

CHAPTER SEVENTEEN

THE RORY FACTOR

If there are two questions you can guarantee Rickie Fowler will be asked more than any others, they are these: 'What do you think of Rory McIlroy?' and 'Is he your biggest rival?' And it is remarkable how the pair are well matched in similarities, career projectories and strong ambitions. For starters, both are of similar age – Rickie was born on 13 December, 1988, and Rory arrived in this world on 4 May, 1989. Then, both are seen as the flag bearers for their nation's golfing hopes for the future – Rory is British while Rickie is American. And both have followed similar career paths and played competitively against each other from a young age. And both have a growing army of fans who loyally follow their fortunes around the world. And both are seen as beacons of a new era of golf – scandal-free, fresh and bringing a much-needed innocent youth and fresh wind of vigour after the excesses of Tiger Woods.

Woods himself was once – and for a considerable length of time – seen as the man who would take the sport to a massive new level of success and open it up to a younger audience. And, to be fair, he did just that – until the truth about his excesses off the greens were revealed. At that stage, the baton passed on to Rickie and Rory. Of course, the young men were rivals for the sport's biggest prizes – but they were also friends on and away from the golf clubs. They were a much-needed, and much-welcome, breath of fresh air.

And given their youth and talent – and the fact that one was British and one was American – it is hardly surprising that Rickie and Rory came to be seen as the new figureheads of a transatlantic race to the top of the golfing world. Taking a look at Rory's background and development, it is revealing to learn just how similar their routes to golfing immortality have been. As this book was completed in December, 2014, the only real stand-out difference between the duo was that Rory had won Majors while Rickie was still attempting to do just that. Few pundits would suggest that Rickie will never do so; most were convinced that it was just a matter of time as he kept knocking on the door and upping the level of his game. And Rory would be one of the first in the golfing fraternity who would tell you that it was a matter of when, not if, as far as Rickie lifting that maiden Major trophy was concerned.

What I also like about Rickie and Rory is that they are genuine nice guys who are generous with their time when it comes to fans and even the media and that they both have a real altruistic side: both are devoted to charity work and helping others less fortunate than themselves. They both set a great example, both are model pros and both are consistent role models for the younger fans they have lured to the game as a result of their success and their efforts to throw golf open to everyone. No longer is it merely the domain of an elite, rich cabal of older men. Rickie and Rory have welcomed everyone – no matter their colour, creed or wealth – to join them in this wonderful, uplifting sport.

Both also enjoyed the staunch and loyal support of family and friends as they moved up the ranks. Both enjoyed a happy childhood and both prospered in the sport with the encouragement of friends and family in their formative years. It was telling, for instance, that when Rory won his first Major – the US Open in 2011 – he immediately ran over to his father Gerry and the two hugged. The triumph was the culmination of two decades' work finally completed. Rory then paid tribute to his father and all the efforts he had put in – the tripling-up on jobs to help him fund his career, the long journeys to different courses and the constant encouragement – by dedicating the victory to him on Father's Day. He said, 'Happy Father's Day, dad – this one's for you,' after proudly showing off his winning trophy at the course in Maryland.

Rory then added, 'But I have to mention my mum as well, who's back home watching. I can't thank them enough. As Graeme [McDowell] said last year there will be a few pints of the black stuff going down tonight. I know my friends will be out partying and I can't wait to get back and join them. But the whole week has been incredible. I knew what

I needed to do today to win. I put a few new things into practice and it paid off.'

Gerry would later reveal that he was 'over the moon' for his son and say that every sacrifice he and wife Rosie had made was now more than worthwhile. He said:

We worked very hard to get him where he is. If we had not put the effort in at the time I could be sitting here wondering what would have happened, and regretting not doing it. It was expensive – hotels, air fares and everything. But we worked to get where we are. We are very lucky with Rory.

Of course there are times everyone gets fed up working, but as the years went by Rory got better and better, so it was more of an incentive. I didn't mind and Rosie didn't mind. Rory is our only child so you can just do the best you can for them. We didn't know what was going to happen. All we did was try our best for him. He drove it all, we just helped him. You can't push kids into anything. But once he decided he wanted to do it, we were 100 per cent behind him.

Gerry's words and obvious delight would bring to mind the same joy Rickie and his folks shared when he won his first PGA trophy at the Wells Fargo in 2012. Gerry also revealed that his now world-famous son was not motivated by money – much the same as Rickie again. Rickie had always maintained he did it for 'the fun of it', not the material gains.

Of course, no one would deny that the winnings had their benefits in terms of lifestyle choices. But it was not the be-all and end-all. Golf was there to be enjoyed as far as the two youngsters were concerned.

Gerry would add, 'Rory has no interest in money. Rory is just Rory. People find it hard to understand, but he doesn't care about cash as long as he has enough to do him. Even growing up he never really cared about money, it has never meant anything to him. He has a nice house nearby and he's put a few quid into it, but apart from that he doesn't spend much.'

Like Rickie, Rory was building up a sizeable fortune, despite it not being his main motivation. His win at the Congressional earned him a cheque for $1.44 million (£900,000). But by becoming the youngest player to win a Major since Tiger Woods lifted the Masters trophy in 1997, he also set himself up for major riches off the green with sponsorship deals. He already pocketed an estimated $10 million in endorsement deals with Dubai hotels group Jumeirah, Titleist who supplied his golf balls, and equipment and sunglasses maker Oakley.

And experts predicted he could double that when the deals came up for renewal – and then there were new deals that would inevitably be put on the table for his inspection. Woods had earned $92 million in sponsorship in 2009 before his bubble burst – so the 'sky's the limit for Rory' according to the experts. One PR exec, Adrian Rogers, said, 'Rory can step into the gap that has been created by Tiger's demise. He has everything the sport is looking for. He is clean, young, attractive and he connects with the public – which is something Tiger really rarely did even at the peak of his powers. Tiger is the past; Rory is the future.'

And so was Rickie. He was also winning new sponsorship deals with each passing year and win. As we have touched upon, he had deals for his own brand of clothing as well as the normal ones for the gear he used. Like Rory, Rickie was clean, young and attractive – but on the other side of the Atlantic from his Irish pal.

Rickie had long spoken of his desire to become one of golf's greats – and how the thought of that motivated him to do his best at every event on the circuit, no matter if it was the smallest or the biggest. And after his US Open win, Rory also freely admitted he would 'love to dominate the sport' as his boyhood hero Tiger Woods had. He had always said that he wanted to emulate Tiger's masterclass of 2000 when he won the U.S. Open by a record fifteen shots at Pebble Beach. Now Rory said, 'I know how good Tiger was in 2000 to win by 15 in Pebble. I was trying to go out there and emulate him. I grew up watching him dominate at the Masters in '97, watching him dominate at Pebble in 2000 and St Andrews. And I was just trying to go out there with the same intensity.

'To get one out of the way early, you can always call yourself a Major champion. And, hopefully, in the not so distant future, I'll be able to call myself a multiple Major champion.'

Rickie was always aware of his fans and that they should be treated well. He made a point of talking with them and signing autographs. He liked them being around and always spoke in glowing terms of them: he insisted on always making time for them, however tight the schedule he was on. Similarly, Rory had a great relationship with his fans – and they loved him too. They told him so on the chat sites and golf sites. After his win at Congressional, they chipped in with a variety of tributes – including one who made the point that Rory's emergence signalled that much-vaunted, and much-needed, changing of the guard at the very top of the sport. The fan said:

Firstly, the most unbelievable display of golf, power, control, imagination, everything I've ever seen – bar nothing Woods has done, and that's saying something. Second, it's a matter of time before McIlroy gets to No. 1, probably after he wins at St George's next month.

Third, it's so refreshing to see what's happening in the sport, after a decade of players happy to tag along in Woods's slipstream, making a million for finishing 100th on tour (not their fault, it's only human nature). Now a batch of kids who had Woods as their hero are bursting on the scene and gunning for HIM like he gunned for Jack.

Woods is history – he may well win another Major, but he's history in more ways than one. Nobody cares about him any more, not Rory, Schwartzel, Oosthuizen, Kaymer, Donald, Mannasero, Ishikawa or another host of 19–23-year-olds in white belts, pounding it for miles and putting like God. Think of your own club – how much better is it when 'the best player' is a nice guy, humble when he wins, gracious when he loses, than a brat who nobody likes but has talent to waste. Woods can leave the scene anytime he likes … and leave the way for a whole new crop who respect the game and more importantly respect each other while trying their hearts out. Sit back and enjoy the next five years – it's been a long time coming.

I couldn't have put that better myself! Rory and Rickie were the new public faces of golf. And both had worked hard from a young age to reach the summit.

'He was holding a golf club before he could walk,' Rory's mother Rose would say. 'He'd be sitting in the pram with a plastic golf club in his hand. That's the way we were woken up: banged over the head with a plastic golf club.' Rosie knew that her son was a special one; that he had golfing genius in his blood from the day he was born in Northern Ireland. And that her husband was quite correct in encouraging him toward the sport from infancy.

As with Rickie, family links and values meant the world to Rory. His father Gerry McIlroy, then twenty-seven, had married Rosaleen McDonald, also twenty-seven, in St Colmcille's Church, in Holywood, East Belfast, County Down, on 13 January, 1988. A year-and-a-half later – on 4 May, 1989 – their son Rory was born, also in Holywood, and would be baptised in the church in which they had wed. He would be their only child and would show glimpses from the age of ten months of the God-given talent bestowed upon him; they would be proud of him and devote themselves through the years to helping him make his dream of becoming a pro golfer come true.

And just as Rickie's family made sacrifices to help him in his chosen career, so would Rory's parents. Gerry would work up to a hundred hours a week in three jobs, cleaning toilets and showers at a local rugby club in the mornings and bartending at the golf club in the afternoons and evenings – and Rosie would clock-on for the night shift at a local factory, packaging millions of rolls of tape.

Back in his days as a toddler, they sent Rory to St Patrick's, a Catholic primary school, where, to this day, his first Communion photograph still hangs on a wall. Rory was a happy child and would later admit he had a contented childhood, mostly oblivious to the sectarian 'Troubles' that had haunted the nation for decades. His parents were determined that he would not become scarred by them and that he would grow up as a young man who was a credit to his nation; and who could cross the Protestant/Catholic divide and bigotry. They did a good job. He grew up with their teachings – of peace and people working as one rather than bitterly divided – and refused to be defined by the fact that he was a Catholic. He would one day admit that one of his major wishes was to be viewed as someone who had overcome all the traditional wranglings of Catholic and Protestant, Irish and British.

Of course, as he grew up, just five miles away in the centre of Belfast the scene was much different – with daily riots and bombs going off – from the relative peace of Holywood. But the McIlroy family would still have their own personal reminder of the Troubles that raged in their homeland. Seventeen years before Rory was born, in 1972, his great-uncle Joe was murdered for moving into a Protestant area of East Belfast by a UVF hit squad. He lies in the same church in which Rory was baptised and Gerry and Rosie were married.

Rory was shielded to a large extent from the Troubles by the very fact that he was lucky enough to grow up in Holywood. It was a small, quintessentially middle-class coastal town with just over 12,000 inhabitants and Rory would enjoy a happy childhood. Gerry was determined that his boy would have chances in life that he and his family had not been granted. The political commentator Newton Emerson best summed up how Rory lived near the Troubles – but had managed not to be personally directly affected by them – when he wrote in *The Irish Times*:

It is just five miles from Rory McIlroy's house in Holywood to the riot-torn streets of East Belfast, yet it might as well be a world away. Nowhere else in the world has a young champion golfer ever lived this close to a riot, except when Tiger Woods lived in Hollywood during the 1993 LA riots. So strictly speaking a young champion golfer has never lived in a town called Holywood with one 'L' just five miles from a riot. But still, picture the contrast between the young man playing golf and the young men throwing golf balls. Powerful stuff.

Rory's dad had a feeling that his boy's big break in life might well be in the game of golf: the game he and his family had adored for many years. Their devotion to golf began with Rory's grandfather Jimmy, who worked repairing cranes in Belfast docks, where the *Titanic* was built. Jimmy played at the Holywood club that has now become synonymous with young Rory's success. He was one of their top players and his enthusiasm washed off on his sons – Rory's father, Gerry, and his uncles Colm and Brian – to also take up golf. Gerry, like Jimmy, would prove the man to beat – a natural and a man who spent hours dedicating himself to improving his game. Gerry would now become the driving force behind his own son's ambitious bid to become the best golfer in the world, let alone Holywood. It was a mission that would not have been possible but for the efforts of Gerry and Rosie – as Rory himself would admit after he won the US Open in 2011.

The mission would begin as soon as Rory could crawl and would end with that remarkable win at the Congressional nearly twenty-two years later. When Rory was born Gerry was already working as a barman at the Holywood golf club – a job that had the perk of allowing him to indulge his own love of golf. Some days Gerry would bring young Rory with him when he went to work and, when he finished his shift and ventured on to the greens, Rory would look on from his pram as his dad hit balls around the course.

Before he was a year old Rory was crawling around the green, following his dad's progress and within another year was driving everyone mad with his own set of plastic clubs and balls. By the age of eighteen months Gerry was already busy teaching him about the game and the toddler would often practise at his great-aunt Frances McDonald's home in Scarva Road, Banbridge. Indeed one of the first pictures of the boy who would become a golfing superstar in action was taken there, on her back lawn, by Frances. 'He first played with his wee putter on my back lawn,' she would later say. 'I remember him well in that wee Aran jumper. He could barely hold the club.'

By the age of two he was hitting forty-yard drives and, although Rory also liked to play football with his mates on the street corner outside his home in Holywood, golf would remain his first love. Soon the golf would become the number one factor in his life as he started to spend more time at Holywood Golf Club (which he still retains as his home course to this day and credits with providing an ideal base to become a top player). Soon, he was being proposed for club membership and, at the tender age of eight, became Holywood's youngest-ever member. 'Everyone at the club knew him by then,' says a source close to the club. 'And everyone knew he was a prodigy – and a potential genius in the making. We knew we were witnessing something very special with this young boy, it was an exciting time.'

Just as Rickie leaned on his trainer Barry McDonnell – who taught him how to swing from an early age – so Rory started his early training with Michael Bannon, the former head golf pro at the club. 'I suppose when he was about five or six you sort of knew there was something special there,' Bannon would say. 'And he was so good when he was seven-and-a-half years of age that one of the men in the golf club came out and asked me what do you think of Rory? Can he join the golf club? ... So Holywood Golf Club let him become a member at eight years of age.'

Robert Cooley, sixty-two, a member of the club for twenty-five years, would later tell the *Daily Mail*, 'His talent was recognised at such a very young age. You could see there was something special there. He had a self-determination that from an early age to wanted to be a golf professional, not only a golf professional, he wanted to be the best golf professional. He could drive the ball forever, chip the ball better, he was a great putter. He has an analytical brain and he has the mettle and fortitude to be the best.'

Like Rickie, Rory was well liked and did well at school. Rory's teachers were amazed when they learned what a golfing prodigy they had in their midst – especially when he won the Under 10 World Championship at Doral in Florida while finishing the course with five shots less than any of the other eighty youngsters taking part!

Such trips abroad did not come cheaply – and this is where Gerry and Rosie's devotion to their son with hard work really started to count. Rory was already making a name for himself – but was also proving a real student of the game at such an early age. He watched endless tournaments with Gerry on the TV and studied the techniques of his favourite golfers – men like Nick Faldo – on videos. He was always eager to learn and digest as much information as he could: instinctively, he knew from an early age that if he was going to be the best he would have to work hard at his game and take in as many tips on how to improve it as he could.

At nine years old, Rory notched his first hole-in-one and also starred on a Northern Ireland TV show, hitting golf balls into a washing machine – just as he was now regularly doing at home (much to his mum Rosie's bemusement!). A year later he would bemuse the pros at Holywood by filling out his own scorecards at Holywood – after he had put a copy of his hero Tiger Woods's scorecard from the 1997 Masters on to his bedroom wall (along with a poster of the number one player of that time).

He would sign the cards 'Rory Nick Faldo McIlroy' in a salute to another of his favourite golfing stars. 'The thing about Rory is when he was growing up and you asked him questions, he'd give you these very definite straight answers and it was stuff ... you couldn't laugh,' Michael Bannon would tell *ESPN*, 'Well, I never did because I always knew someday this guy could do it.'

Rickie became renowned for his skills with a golf ball through high school and college. Similarly, when the time came for Rory to step up to secondary school, he moved to Sullivan Upper – a religiously mixed grammar school. Gerry and Rosie had been impressed by its values and motto, which is printed on pupils' blazers: Lámh Foisdineach An Uachtar. This is Irish for 'with the gentle hand foremost' – and served to support their ambition of Rory growing up in a new Northern Ireland, one forged through peaceful means, one in which conflict and the bomb and the gun had no place to thrive.

Rory settled into his new school and continued to prove more adept at golf than his lessons. Aged eleven, he shot level par at Holywood Golf Club and then spent the summer of 2000 playing the game in America. He took part in ten junior tournaments organised by the Utah Junior Golf Association – and didn't win any of them! Rory had met a boy called Scott Pinckney when he won the Under 10 World Championship in Florida the previous year. Scott had told him all about the events in Utah and Rory had pestered Gerry and Rosie to allow him to go over to the States for the summer. Eventually they relented, keen to allow their son to develop as a person and a golfer, and he stayed with Scott's family.

Just as Rickie enjoyed his summers as a boy, biking and golfing, so Rory had a great summer despite failing to win on his Florida vacation. By the age of thirteen Rory was a scratch handicap golfer and by fifteen he and his parents began to seriously examine his options. Should he stay on at school beyond sixteen and try to achieve academic success? Or would he be better served leaving early and concentrating on a golfing career that was already suggesting massive rewards? He was no academic genius, but he was no dunce either. But he was a golfing genius, no doubt about it.

Rickie would choose to leave his college and follow his dream of becoming a golf pro, so Rory too would choose to opt out early in the summer of 2005, just before taking his GCSEs – it was a brave decision and one that would pay huge dividends. A brave decision that was quite logical when you considered just how brilliant he was at the game of golf. Talking years later about his time at Sullivan, Rory would tell youngsters at the school, 'A few of the teachers will tell you I probably wasn't the best pupil you've ever seen.' He admitted that he found it difficult to concentrate on schoolwork, given his dedication to golf, saying: 'It was tough. I was away quite a lot so every time I came back I was always trying to catch up. It was very tough to try to balance everything, but I tried my best. All I wanted to do was play golf and I knew by the time I was fifteen or sixteen that that was the path I was going to take.'

And, like Rickie, the path they both decided to take was the correct one. As Rickie quickly started to make a name for himself on the amateur circuit, so too did Rory. The Irishman had only just celebrated his sixteenth birthday when he shocked the pros with his showing at Royal Portrush – which had hosted the 1951 Open – on the north coast of Northern Ireland. He was taking part in the North of Ireland Amateur Open at the world-famous course in July 2005 when he hit an 11-under-par round of 61. That amazing round included nine birdies and an eagle – and it bettered the previous record by three shots.

Naturally, Rory was delighted with his round, labelling it 'unbelievable'. 'To shoot 61 anywhere is great – but to shoot it around Royal Portrush is even better,' he told the BBC. 'It was a great experience.' Dese Hassan of Royal Portrush, put a more perceptive angle on it when he said: 'It was a marvellous performance by anybody. But for a sixteen-year-old boy to go round one of the major links in the world in 61 shots – 33 out and 28 back and 26 putts – is phenomenal.' It was the round that pushed him into the limelight – from now on no one would ask who he was or if he had the potential to be a great.

On 6 February 2007 Rory would top the World Amateur Golf Ranking, though he lost the top spot after just one week, before regaining it a month later. That number-one spot was reclaimed after his brilliant individual performances in the Grey Goose Cup (formerly known as the Sherry Cup) in Spain. He won the Cup and was thrilled as he had now emulated Padraig Harrington and Sergio Garcia by winning the individual title at the European Nations Championship at Sotogrande. He had opened with a 69 to share second place – in a tie with Marius Thorp of Norway and Belgium's Xavier Feyaerts on three under par, and just one stroke behind Dane Peter Baunsoe.

Rory was just as pleased that the win had put him back at the top of the amateur world rankings – but it had been a tense finish as he triumphed over Thorp in a sudden death situation, ending Ireland's sixteen-year search for a winner (the last being Harrington in 1991). Rory would not be making it a double cause for celebration: his Irish team lost out by just one stroke for the team title to the Danish, finishing tied second with England.

The Irishman had one more big tournament to play in before he would say goodbye to his amateur status – and it was an event that would finally bring him face to face with Rickie on British soil. Both had worked hard to be selected for the 2007 Walker Cup, but it was Rory who had more pressure on him to do well – as the event was held in his homeland at the Royal County Down club. It was also, the men of the Press would claim, his 'last chance to make an impression on the amateur game' before he joined the ranks of the professionals.

Tony Disley, chairman of the R&A selection committee, said Rory was in there on merit, adding: 'We have picked a strong team that is more than capable of defeating the Americans. The team not only includes players with experience at the highest level but has a number of exciting younger players who we believe will excel on the occasion.' And home captain Colin Dalgleish added, 'Rory has a sound technique and great flair. It's a great and amazing coincidence to have somebody of Rory's exceptional talent to come along when the matches are being played in County Down. We're expecting great things of him, but Rory gets no special privileges.'

The welcome from the thousands of home fans who turned out to greet him would never be forgotten by Rory. 'He was so grateful and appreciative,' a source confirms. 'He loves the fans who get behind him from Northern Ireland and felt a very special bond with them over the two days – as he always does when they turn out for him. It was a very special weekend for him on home territory – it was just a pity that the result didn't match the occasion.'

Rory being Rory, he was one of the first to greet the Americans when they arrived at Royal County Down, and he extended the hand of friendship to Rickie and his teammates. In a pre-tournament press conference, Rory always made it clear that he had been watching Rickie's development across the water as he highlighted him as one of the young men who could cause the hosts problems.

And Rory said, 'They are all good players – they wouldn't be here if they weren't. I played with Kyle Stanley before at the Orange Grove a couple of years ago and Rickie Fowler is another good young player. Jamie Lovemark as well. There are a lot of really good individuals on that team, and it's going to be tough for us this week.'

Indeed it was – Rickie would get one over on Rory as Team USA defeated Team GB & I by a score of 12.5 to 11.5 and it wasn't one of Rory's better days at the office – going 1-2-1 in the competition. In comparison, Rickie's figures were 2–0 in foursomes and 1–1 in singles, making his overall record 3–1. The pair were both 18 and had to wait until the second day of proceedings before they faced each other in the foursomes. Rickie and Billy Horschel beat Rory and Jon Caldwell 2 and 1. Two years later, Rickie would play in the return Walker Cup fixture at Merion in Ardmore, but Rory would be absent. Rickie would be celebrating again as the States retained the trophy with an emphatic victory.

By then, the pro circuit was calling out loud to both men. Rory had turned professional on September 19, 2007. Rickie, as we have noted, had turned pro somewhat later – after the 2009 Walker Cup to be precise. And just as it took Rickie a little time to get used to the pro game and win his first tournament, so Rory would also take time to adjust – and triumph. Sixteen months after turning pro, the Irishman won the Dubai Desert Classic after leading from start to finish and had to see off a fine field. The triumph meant that, at nineteen years and two hundred and seventy-three days, he had become the third youngest player in European Tour history, the youngest player ever to make it into the world top 20 rankings and that he was now ranked fourteenth in the world. Rory was also the youngest winner of the Dubai event, beating the previous best of England's David Howell, who had won the 1999 edition when he was twenty-three years and two hundred and thirty-six days old.

After winning the Dubai Desert Classic on February 1, 2009, Rory would admit that the victory was 'a monkey off my back' – exactly the same words Rickie would use to describe his first pro win at the Wells Fargo in 2012. Rory would add that his main motivation now was to go out and win another tournament as soon as possible – again just like Rickie. 'Your success only makes you more motivated to try to do better,' Rory told reporters. 'I've realised that I've become a very good player and I just want to keep trying to practise harder and improve. It's [the win] definitely a monkey off my back. If I had not won today, having a six-shot lead, it would have been pretty tough to take, and it would have been hard to come back from that. But I was able to scrape in at the end.'

He was asked what he had learned – and if he could put any learning experiences to good use. 'Golf is such a funny game, you can be so far ahead but the guys can still pay you back and that's what happened,' he said. 'Justin [Rose] made a great eagle on 13, great birdie on 17, and my lead was down to one and you have to reassess. But all of these situations and all of these positions that I've put myself in are experience – and I'm gathering it week-by-week. Obviously the experiences that I've had in the past helped me today and hopefully today's will help me in the future.'

Rory was also keen to pay tribute to his mum Rosie and dad Gerry. He said: 'This win is definitely for my parents who were here. They have never been pushy, they have done so much for me, and it's nice to be able to repay them in some way.'

Like Rickie, Rory never forgot where he had come from and the debt he owed to his family. They were the rock he relied upon and were always there for him. Also like Rickie, Rory had a level-headedness about him that boded well for his future. Both young men refused to get carried away by the hype that surrounds the sport and stayed close to family and friends to ensure they stayed grounded. Both were willing to learn from tough experience and were willing to listen to managers and advisers. These were distinct characteristic advantages as they moved ever forward.

Of course some pundits assessed the rivalry only on black and white statistics. They pointed to Rory's multi wins on the circuit and the fact he had won four Majors by the end of 2014. In contrast, Rickie had one win and no Majors to his name. Within that framework, yes, you could argue that Rory was roaring ahead (excuse the pun). But Rickie was closing the gap fast and few pundits and fellow golfers (including Rory) believed that he would not join Rory in lifting Major trophies.

Rickie was a work in progress; he moved at his own pace but each tournament and each month edged him closer to the big ones – the wins that would silence the doubters once and for all.

The young American golfer himself is determined to close the gap and has the self-belief to to do just that. After he beat Rory to the Korea Open title in 2010 – his first pro win – Rickie admitted that getting one over on Rory was something to savour, saying, 'He's beaten me, I've beaten him before, but to win a golf tournament and beat him was different. It was cool.' He accepts that Rory is in command just now, recently saying, 'I definitely have some catching up to do. But I am getting closer.' Indeed he is – and I would not be at all surprised if he pulls off a big one – maybe even winning the Masters as his first Major scalp!

As this book went to the printers, Rory and Rickie – still both in their mid-twenties – could afford to laugh as the pundits predicted theirs is the rivalry that will define Anglo-American golf for the next couple of decades. But behind the smiles, both know it is probably correct. Yes, the era of R&R is definitely upon us.